COMPUTERISED ACCOUNTS FOR
City & Guilds
Levels 1 and 2
Pitmans

Nicola Antoni

Liberty Hall
Limited

Educational Publishers

ISBN 1 84224 317 9

Computerised Accounts for C&G Levels 1 and 2 (PITMANS)
Published by Liberty Hall Ltd

© Copyright Liberty Hall Ltd, 2005

ISBN 1 84224 317 9

A CIP catalogue record for this book is available. from the British Library

Second Edition 2005

Printed by Liberty Hall Ltd

Acknowledgements

Window screen images and icons reprinted with permission from Sage.

To my friends for their help and my husband for his patience

The author

Nicola Antoni is a fellow of the Chartered Association of Certified Accountants and has worked for many years in private practice.

At present she is a lecturer in Accounting at a Sixth Form College.

Liberty Hall Ltd is a publishing company producing books for students of IT, Computing and Business.

Liberty Hall believes that:

- Education is the key to freedom.

- Good education is achieved through good teaching.

- Good teaching is supported by sound educational material.

- Books should be designed for the students.

- Books should be affordable.

Liberty Hall's books are written by good, experienced teachers who share these values.

CONTENTS

INTRODUCTION

This book has been designed specifically for City and Guilds (formerly Pitmans) Bookkeeping and Accounts Level 1 and Level 2. These awards can either be gained as a unitised provision in their own right or combined with Computerised Accounts Level 1 and 2 respectively to achieve a Level 1 or 2 Certificate in Accounting.

The fundamentals of basic bookkeeping are identical, the difference is created by the medium used to record the information i.e. manual or computerised. It is therefore recommended very strongly that the elementary principles are learnt in a manual environment prior to using a computerised one.

It is of course possible to press buttons on a keyboard and obtain results without the underlying knowledge, but this will not provide the necessary understanding for these results to be meaningful and thus be of use to the business. Similarly it will not be possible to sort out any difficulties or problems encountered and worse still inaccuracies will not be identified.

The real test of understanding comes when things do not go as expected but the knowledge gained is capable of resolving the issue both confidently and competently. Thus this book aims to provide the reader with the requisite tools to master the basics of bookkeeping and accounts at levels 1 and 2.

Chapter 1	The Accounting System

Objectives
By the end of the Chapter you will be able to describe

☐   The Accounting System

1.1   The Accounting System

The accounting system is the process of recording financial information from its starting point, financial documents, through to the generation of the final accounts. There are five stages, which are outlined below:

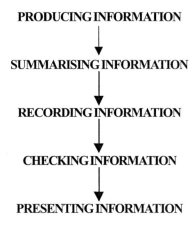

PRODUCING INFORMATION

↓

SUMMARISING INFORMATION

↓

RECORDING INFORMATION

↓

CHECKING INFORMATION

↓

PRESENTING INFORMATION

1.2   Producing Information

This relates to the production of the relevant documents that are involved in the purchase and sale of goods and services e.g. invoices. Businesses will produce many documents on a daily basis. It is therefore essential that they keep track of them. In order to do so they must gather them together and summarise the information.

1.3   Summarising Information

So that the information contained within the documents can be processed, all documents of the same type e.g. sales invoices, are collected together. Once this has taken place they are summarised in the day books e.g. sales day book of the business. Day books are so called as businesses can enter the document details on a daily basis. Thus if a business issues five sales invoices on one day, they will put them in a batch all together and enter them into the day books at the end of the day. As this is the first place that the financial transactions have been recorded day books are also called books of original entry.

1.4   Recording Information

The information listed in the day books has to be transferred by a process known as double entry bookkeeping into the main business accounts, which are contained within the ledgers Traditionally ledgers were leather bound books in which the details were entered manually but often these days ledgers are part of an accounting software package with the details being entered using a computer. As with the day books there are ledgers for different transactions e.g. sales ledger

1.5   Checking Information

The information in the ledger accounts is checked by extracting a trial balance. A trial balance is a summary of all the transactions that have been entered into the ledger. All the ledger accounts will be balanced. This means that the difference between the two sides of the account is worked out and shown as a balancing figure. By extracting the balances on the ledger accounts and putting them into a trial balance, it is possible to check the accuracy of the debit and credit entries made when recording the information.

Once the trial balance has been extracted and it has been confirmed that it balances, it can be used to prepare the final accounts.

1.5   Presenting Information

The final accounts consist of two documents, a trading and profit and loss account and a balance sheet. The trading and profit and loss account shows how much profit or loss has been made by the business whilst the balance sheet shows what is owned and owed by the business.

The trial balance contains all the essential information. In order to prepare the final accounts it is necessary to identify the balances that belong to the trading and profit and loss account and those that belong to the balance sheet.

Chapter 2	Financial Documents
	(Producing Information)

Objectives
By the end of the Chapter you will be able to describe

☐   financial documents

2.1   Introduction

Whenever an item is bought or sold a business transaction occurs. An exchange takes place of goods or services and in return money or a promise to pay at a later date is received. Thus business transactions are of two main types: **cash**, where settlement occurs immediately and **credit**, where payment occurs at some point in the future. Note that cash refers to all payments that are made straight away whether by cash, cheque, credit or debit card. Credit however means that the goods have changed hands but no monetary exchange has yet taken place but is anticipated to occur at a later date mutually agreed by the parties to the transaction.

2.2   Financial Documents

All financial transactions generate documents. These documents are the 'starting point' in an accounting system for a business. They contain details of the transactions that the business has undertaken and need to be entered into the accounting records of the business. They are also called source documents because they are the source of all the information recorded by a business.

Whenever a business buys or sells goods or services on **credit** financial documents must be prepared. Therefore all businesses must know which financial documents they are required to produce and the sequence they need to complete them. The first and last documents flow from the buyer (the person who requires the goods) to the seller (the person who has the goods) whereas those documents in between flow from the seller to the buyer. The relevant documents are:

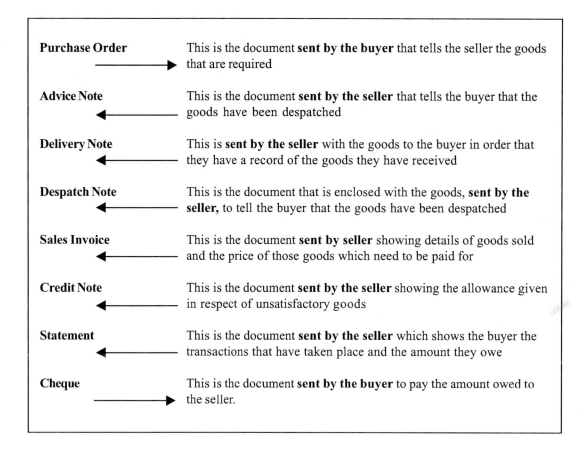

Purchase Order	This is the document **sent by the buyer** that tells the seller the goods that are required
Advice Note	This is the document **sent by the seller** that tells the buyer that the goods have been despatched
Delivery Note	This is **sent by the seller** with the goods to the buyer in order that they have a record of the goods they have received
Despatch Note	This is the document that is enclosed with the goods, **sent by the seller,** to tell the buyer that the goods have been despatched
Sales Invoice	This is the document **sent by seller** showing details of goods sold and the price of those goods which need to be paid for
Credit Note	This is the document **sent by the seller** showing the allowance given in respect of unsatisfactory goods
Statement	This is the document **sent by the seller** which shows the buyer the transactions that have taken place and the amount they owe
Cheque	This is the document **sent by the buyer** to pay the amount owed to the seller.

Not all of these documents will be used by every business e.g. a credit note will only be issued when a buyer is unhappy with goods and the seller is in agreement i.e. the goods are faulty. Many businesses will not have advice notes, delivery notes and despatch notes but may combine them e.g. despatch/advice note or send the invoice with the goods and use it as a despatch note as well.

The sequence of documents described above assumes that goods and services have been bought on credit i.e. buy now, pay later.

When goods and services are sold on a **cash** basis, the buyer and the seller will require documentation to prove that the transaction has taken place. As soon as the goods are transferred payment is made immediately, by cash cheque or credit card thereby the only document required is evidence that the buyer has acquired the goods in exchange for payment. This is called a receipt that may be produced by a till or it may be hand-written.

Finally a document used specifically as an authorisation form for small cash items of expenditure is a petty cash voucher.

Chapter 3

Day Books (Summarising Information)

3

Objectives

By the end of the Chapter you will be able to describe

☐ day books

3.1 Introduction

As can be seen above, there are many different types of documents relating to business transactions. It is therefore necessary to gather together all documents of the same type e.g. sales transactions, purchases transactions or money transactions.

Sales transactions can be split into sales and sales returns transactions, as can purchases into purchases and purchases returns transactions. These will be recorded into different day books as follows:

Day Book	Document
Sales day book – for credit sales	Sales invoices
Sales returns day book – for credit sales returns	Sales credit notes
Purchase day book – for credit purchases	Purchase invoices
Purchase returns day book – for credit purchase returns	Purchase credit notes
Cash book – for receipts and payments of cash	Cheques, paying-in slips, receipts
Petty cash book	Petty cash vouchers, receipts

3.2 Sales Day Book

Below is the sales day book of A J Dowle

Sales Day Book			
Date	Details	Invoice Number	Total £
1 Jan	James Lloyd	158369	315.00
3 Jan	Frank Jones	158370	400.00
4 Jan	Wilson Bros	158371	600.00
6 Jan	Frank Jones	158372	100.00
7 Jan	Totals for week		1415.00

The sales day book (shown on the previous page) contains the following information

- · ● date of transaction

- · ● account name

- · ● invoice number

- · ● amount of transaction

As each invoice is issued it will be dated and the date on the invoice is recorded in the day book. In this case these invoices have been issued in the first week of January.

All invoices should have their own unique identification number. These need to be shown. As sales invoices are issued by the seller the numbers will be consecutive. In the example above the invoice numbers are 158369 to 158372.

The sales day book lists the invoices that have been issued to buyers i.e. customers who have had their goods on credit. Thus the name of the person who owes the business money needs to be shown. It enables the particular invoice to be identified, together with the date and invoice number. In the example above the customers are James Lloyd, Frank Jones and Wilson Bros.

The amount of the invoice is shown in the total column and at the end of the period, be it daily, weekly or monthly the column is totalled and the relevant date, and appropriate narrative e.g. "totals for week" (or month) is added. Trade discount may be shown which is a reduction given to a customer when calculating the selling price of goods but, it is the net amount that is shown in the day book e.g. unit price £12.50, trade discount 10% so net price £11.25 (£12.50 - £1.25 = £11.25)

3.3 Purchase Day Book

A purchase day book is identical to a sales day book except that the invoice numbers are not sequential. The invoices are received from various different sellers i.e. suppliers who all have their own system for creating their invoice numbers.

Below is the purchases day book of A J Dowle

Date	Details	Invoice Number	Net £
1 Jan	Apples Galore	WSE145	500.00
2 Jan	Beautiful Bottles	378931	200.00
4 Jan	Apples Galore	WSE 163	150.00
5 Jan	Dome & Son	I2554367	50.00
7 Jan	Totals for week		900.00

3.4 Returns Day Book

Both sales returns day books and purchases returns day books are identical to the day books above except that they have fewer entries as hopefully more goods are kept than returned! Also the invoice number has been replaced with credit note number.

Below is the sales returns day book of A J Dowle

Sales Returns Day Book

Date	Details	Credit Note Number	Net £
2 Jan	James Lloyd	275	15.00
7 Jan	Totals for week		15.00

Below is the purchases returns day book of A J Dowle.

Purchases Returns Day Book

Date	Details	Credit Note Number	Net £
3 Jan	Beautiful Bottles	132	20.00
7 Jan	Totals for week		20.00

3.5 Cash Book

The cash book is a record kept in date order of all monies actually received or paid out by the business during an accounting period. As monies can be in the form of either cash or cheque, the cash book has two separate columns called cash and bank. It is a book of original entry as it provides a summary of the relevant source documents e.g. receipts, paying-in slips and cheques.

Below is the cash book of A J Dowle for one week:

Cash Book

Date	Details	Cash £	Bank £	Date	Details	Cash £	Bank £
1 Jan	Capital		3000.00	1 Jan	Rent		750.00
2 Jan	Sales		330.00	1 Jan	Purchases		900.00
4 Jan	Sales	480.00		1 Jan	Equipment		760.00
5 Jan	Cash (contra)		200.00	5 Jan	Bank (contra)	200.00	
				5 Jan	Wages	180.00	
				5 Jan	Drawings		500.00

Please note the difference between drawings and wages. Wages is paid to staff working for the owner whereas drawings are taken by the owner themselves.

3.6   Petty Cash Book

Petty cash is money held in cash, in order to meet small items of expenditure where a cheque would not be appropriate e.g. milk bills, taxis, stamps, In order to reduce the number of entries in the main cash book, these items are recorded in a petty cash book. To keep the cash secure it is kept usually in a locked tin.

Below is the petty cash book of A J Dowle for one week:

Receipts £	Date	Details	Voucher	Total £	Travel £	Stationery £	Postage £	Cleaning £
		Petty Cash Book						
50.00	1 Jan	Cash Introduced						
	1 Jan	New Petty Cash Book	001	12.50		12.50		
	2 Jan	Postage Stamps	002	7.00			7.00	
	3 Jan	Taxi Fare	003	3.00	3.00			
	5 Jan	Cleaning Materials	004	5.00				5.00
	6 Jan	Envelopes	005	2.50		2.50		

Thus the day books are used to list the transactions which have taken place in the business. Now that the transactions have been summarised, they need to be recorded into the **ledgers** of the business

Chapter 4 | Double Entry Bookkeeping (Recording Information)

Objectives
By the end of the Chapter you will be able to describe

☐   double entry bookkeeping

4.1 | Introduction

The information listed in the day books has to be transferred into the main business accounts, which are contained within the ledgers. The ledgers are:

- sales ledger

- purchase ledger

- nominal ledger (also called general ledger)

- cash book

- petty cash book (not all businesses will have a petty cash book)

4.2 | The Sales Ledger

The sales ledger contains an account for all the customers (buyers) who have been sold goods on credit. The business needs a record of the customers that owe money and the amount that they owe. When the customer pays at a later date this will also be recorded in the sales ledger. These accounts relate to people and are called personal accounts.

4.3 | The Purchase Ledger

Names of the suppliers (sellers) that the business has bought goods from on credit are contained within the purchase ledger. The business will need to know the suppliers to whom money is owed and the amount of the debt. A record of the payment to the supplier at a later date will be recorded in the purchase ledger. As with the sales ledger, accounts in the purchase ledger relate to people and are personal accounts.

4.4 Nominal Ledger

All other accounts (except for cash – see below) are located in the nominal ledger. Each account is given a specific name and a number for reference purposes They are called impersonal accounts. These related to the following:

expenses of the business e.g. rent and rates
revenue of the business e.g. sales income and commission received
items that the business owns (assets) e.g. property and equipment.
items that the business owes (liabilities) e.g. loans and mortgages
capital – money from the owner

Those impersonal accounts that relate to things e.g. property are called real accounts whereas those impersonal accounts which are "in name only" i.e. nominal such as rent are called nominal accounts.

4.5 Cash Book

The cash book contains a record of cash and bank transactions. It shows all the money, cash or cheques that is received by the business and the payments that are made by the business. The cash book acts as both a book of prime entry (as shown in 3.5) and as a ledger and thus entering items in the cash book represents part of the double entry system as well.

4.6 Petty Cash Book

The petty cash book is used to record the cash received, this being predominantly the imprest top up amount (left hand side) and the payments made (right hand side). The imprest system is used for petty cash, which means there is a maximum amount of money in petty cash that is refunded at regular intervals e.g. weekly once payments have been made. The payments are analysed between the various categories of expenditure.

4.7 Double Entry Bookkeeping

The information is entered into the ledgers to show the effect of the transactions and is undertaken by a process known as double entry bookkeeping. Double entry simply means that a transaction is entered twice in the ledger accounts as each transaction has a two fold effect. The two sides are called debit (left hand side) and credit (right hand side).

The **debit** side is the **IN** side, it is the side which gains value in money, goods or services flowing into the business.

The **credit** side is the **OUT** side; it is the side, which gives value money, goods or services flowing out of the business.

Cash transactions

With goods and services sold on a cash basis, as soon as the goods are transferred payment is made immediately. The twofold effect is that:

The debit side has goods that it did not have before i.e. increase

The credit side has less cash than it had before i.e. decrease

Illustration 4.1

A J Dowle sells six bottles of Sussex Cider to Mrs Langrish for £30.00 cash and issues her a receipt. In double entry terms the following occurred:

The debit side has **cash** of £30.00 that it did not have before i.e. increase

The credit side has six **bottles** less than it had before i.e. decrease

debit	Cash A/C	credit		debit	Cider Sales A/C	credit
6 Bottles £30.00 of cider						Cash £30.00

The cash account would be located in the **Cash Book**.

The cider sales account would be located in the **Nominal Ledger**.

Credit Transactions

If the bottles of cider had been bought on credit the position would have been slightly different.

Illustration 4.2

This time A J Dowle sells 6 bottles of cider for £30.00 to Mrs Langrish on credit terms and issues her a sales invoice. This time payment will be made at some point in the future.

The debit side has **a promise** from the customer Mrs Langrish of £30.00 in the future that it did not have before i.e. increase

The credit side has **six bottles less** than it had before i.e. decrease

debit	Mrs Langrish A/C	credit		debit	Cider Sales A/C	credit
6 Bottles of cider	£30.00					Mrs Langrish £30.00

The Mrs Langrish account would be located in the **Sales Ledger.**

The cider sales account would be located in the **Nominal Ledger.**

Thus the entry in the cider sales account is exactly the same, as the business has acquired the goods in both cases. In Illustration 4.1 the transaction is complete as the money has been received but in Illustration 4.2 the money is still owed by the customer, thus another stage is yet to take place.

Mrs Langrish pays A J Dowle £30.00 the sum owing.

debit	Mrs Langrish A/C		credit		debit	Cider Sales A/C		credit
6 Bottles of cider (original entry)	£30.00	**Cash** (new entry)	**£30.00**				Mrs Langrish (original entry)	£30.00

debit	Cash A/C	credit
Mrs Langrish (new entry)	**£30.00**	

It can be seen that the entries are now the same in the cider sales account £30.00 credit and in the cash account £30.00 debit as in illustration 4.1. In illustration 4.2, however, it was necessary to use the customer's account as the money was not received immediately but at a later date.

Illustration 4.3

Now that the principle of double entry has been explained, the information from the sales day book (reproduced below) can be recorded in the ledger accounts.

Sales Day Book			
Date	**Details**	**InvoiceNumber**	**Total £**
1 Jan	James Lloyd	158369	315.00
3 Jan	Frank Jones	158370	400.00
4 Jan	Wilson Bros	158371	600.00
6 Jan	Frank Jones	158372	100.00
7 Jan	Totals for week		1415.00

The amounts owed by the individual customers will be transferred to the **Sales Ledger** (debit side)

The total sales will be transferred to the **Nominal Ledger** (credit side)

Sales Ledger

James Lloyd		Frank Jones	
1 Jan SDB £315.00		3 Jan SDB £400.00 6 Jan SDB £100.00	

Wilson Bros
_____|_____
4 Jan SDB £600.00 |
                       |
                       |

Nominal Ledger

Sales
_____|_____
                       | 7 Jan SDB £1415.00
                       |
                       |

Please note that SDB is short for Sales Day Book.

Illustration 4.4

Likewise the information from the purchase day book (reproduced below) needs to be recorded in the ledger accounts.

Date	Details	Invoice Number	Net £
1 Jan	Apples Galore	WSE145	500.00
2 Jan	Beautiful Bottles	378931	200.00
4 Jan	Apples Galore	WSE 163	150.00
5 Jan	Dome & Son	I2554367	50.00
7 Jan	Totals for week		900.00

The amounts owed to the individual suppliers will be transferred to the **Purchase Ledger** (credit side)

The total purchases will be transferred to the **Nominal Ledger** (debit side)

Purchase Ledger

Apples Galore
_____|_____
                       | 1 Jan PDB £500.00
                       | 4 Jan PDB £150.00
                       |
                       |

Beautiful Bottles
_____|_____
                       | 2 Jan PDB £200.00
                       |
                       |

Dome & Son
_____|_____
                       | 5 Jan PDB £50.00
                       |
                       |

Nominal Ledger

	Purchases	
7 Jan PDB £950.00		

Please note that PDB is short for Purchase Day Book.

Illustration 4.5

The information from the sales returns day book (reproduced below) needs to be recorded in the ledger accounts.

Sales Returns Day Book			
Date	**Details**	**Credit Note Number**	**Net £**
2 Jan	James Lloyd	275	15.00
7 Jan	Totals for week		15.00

The amounts owed to the individual customer will be transferred to the **Sales Ledger** (credit side)

The total sales returns will be transferred to the **Nominal Ledger** (debit side)

Sales Ledger (from 4.3)   **Nominal Ledger**

James Lloyd		Sales Returns	
1 Jan SDB £315.00	2 Jan SRDB £15.00	2 Jan SRDB £15.00	

James Lloyd's account in the Sales ledger has two entries, one representing the invoice and the other the credit note.

Illustration 4.6

The information will be entered into the ledger accounts from the purchases returns day book as shown below:

Purchases Returns Day Book			
Date	**Details**	**Credit Note Number**	**Net £**
3 Jan	Beautiful Bottles	132	20.00
7 Jan	Totals for week		20.00

Purchases Ledger   **Nominal Ledger**

Beautiful Bottles			Purchases Returns	
3 Jan PRDB £20.00	2 Jan PDB £200.00			3 Jan PRDB £20.00

The amounts due from the individual supplier will be transferred to the **Purchases Ledger** (debit side)

The total purchases returns will be transferred to the **Nominal Ledger** (debit side)

Illustration 4.7

As explained above (4.5), the information from the cash book needs to be entered into the ledger accounts but only one side, as the other side be it debit (receipts) or credit (payments) is already recorded.

Cash Book							
Date	**Details**	**Cash £**	**Bank £**	**Date**	**Details**	**Cash £**	**Bank £**
1 Jan	Capital		3000.00	1 Jan	Rent		750.00
2 Jan	Sales		330.00	1 Jan	Purchases		900.00
4 Jan	Sales	480.00		1 Jan	Equipment		760.00
5 Jan	Cash (contra)		200.00	5 Jan	Wages	180.00	
				5 Jan	Drawings		500.00
				5 Jan	Bank (contra)	200.00	

Nominal Ledger

Capital			Sales	
	1 Jan Bank £3000.00			2 Jan Bank £330.00
				4 Jan Cash £480.00

The monies received are entered (already) in the **Cash Book** (debit side)

The income accounts will be transferred to the **Nominal Ledger** (credit side)

Rent			Purchases	
1 Jan Bank £750.00			1 Jan Bank £900.00	

Equipment			Wages	
1 Jan Bank £760.00			5 Jan Cash £180.00	

Drawings	
5 Jan Bank £500.00	

The monies paid are entered (already) in the **Cash Book** (debit side)

The expenses accounts will be transferred to the **Nominal Ledger** (credit side)

Illustration 4.8

The sales and purchases accounts need to be updated to show the figures from the sales and purchases day books for the week ended 7 January.

Purchases		Sales	
1 Jan Bank £950.00			2 Jan Bank £330.00
7 Jan PDB £900.00			4 Jan Cash £480.00
			7 Jan SDB £1415.00

Illustration 4.9

As with the main cash book, the payments from the petty cash book also need to be entered into the nominal ledger on the debit side only. (the credit side is in the petty cash book). The cash introduced needs to be entered on the credit side of the capital account and the columns need to be totalled.

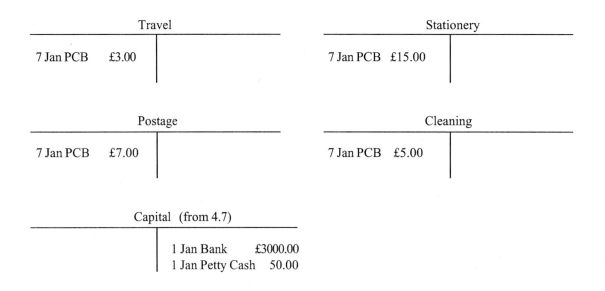

Receipts £	Date	Details	Voucher No	Total £	Travel £	Stationery £	Postage £	Cleaning £
50.00	1 Jan	Cash Introduced						
	1 Jan	New Petty Cash Book	001	12.50		12.50		
	2 Jan	Postage Stamps	002	7.00			7.00	
	3 Jan	Taxi Fare	003	3.00	3.00			
	5 Jan	Cleaning Materials	004	5.00				5.00
	7 Jan	Envelopes	005	2.50		2.50		
				30.00	3.00	15.00	7.00	5.00

Petty Cash Book

Travel		Stationery	
7 Jan PCB £3.00		7 Jan PCB £15.00	

Postage		Cleaning	
7 Jan PCB £7.00		7 Jan PCB £5.00	

Capital (from 4.7)	
	1 Jan Bank £3000.00
	1 Jan Petty Cash 50.00

Illustration 4.10 (from 4.7)

There are also some additional receipts and payments to be shown in the cash book below:

			Cash Book					
Date	**Details**	**Cash £**	**Bank £**		**Date**	**Details**	**Cash £**	**Bank £**
1 Jan	Capital		3000.00		1 Jan	Rent		750.00
2 Jan	Sales		330.00		1 Jan	Purchases		950.00
4 Jan	Sales	480.00			1 Jan	Equipment		760.00
					5 Jan	Wages	180.00	
					5 Jan	Drawings		500.00
5 Jan	**Cash (contra)**		**200.00**		**5 Jan**	**Bank (contra)**	**200.00**	

Firstly on 5 Jan an amount of £200.00 is paid into the bank account out of the cash sales received on 4 January. As can be seen both entries are made in the cash book but the debit entry is in the bank column (money paid IN to the bank) and the credit entry is in the cash column (money paid OUT of cash). Contra has been written in brackets against each entry which signifies that both entries are in the same book.

Illustration 4.11 (from 4.10)

On 6 January £400.00 is received from Frank Jones, a customer whilst the business pays a cheque on the same date of £500.00 to a supplier, Apples Galore. These items are entered into the cash book and the relevant nominal accounts below:

			Cash Book					
Date	**Details**	**Cash £**	**Bank £**		**Date**	**Details**	**Cash £**	**Bank £**
1 Jan	Capital		3000.00		1 Jan	Rent		750.00
2 Jan	Sales		330.00		1 Jan	Purchases		950.00
4 Jan	Sales	480.00			1 Jan	Equipment		760.00
5 Jan	Cash (contra)		200.00		5 Jan	Bank (contra)	200.00	
6 Jan	**Frank Jones**		**400.00**		5 Jan	Wages	180.00	
					5 Jan	Drawings		500.00
					6 Jan	**Apples Galore**		**500.00**

Purchases Ledger

Apples Galore (from 4.4)

6 Jan Bank £500.00	1 Jan PDB £500.00	
	4 Jan PDB £150.00	

The money paid is entered (already) in the **Cash Book** (credit side)

The supplier it is paid to will be entered to the **Purchases Ledger** (debit side)

Sales Ledger

Frank Jones (from 4.3)

3 Jan SDB £400.00	**6 Jan Bank £400.00**
6 Jan SDB £100.00	

The money received is entered (already) in the **Cash Book** (debit side)

The customer it is received from will be entered in the **Sales Ledger** (credit side)

Illustration 4.12

In the above cases the supplier was paid the amount of money owed and the money was received in full from the customer for the outstanding invoice. Sometimes, however, a discount is received from suppliers for prompt payment called discount received. Likewise customers may also be allowed a discount, called discount allowed for prompt payment. This discount is a matter of a business' payments policy and is called cash or settlement discount. It is not to be confused with trade discount which is a matter of a business' trading policy and is not shown in the books. Cash discount is shown in the ledger accounts but is recorded as a memorandum (a note) in the cash book. To do this a three column cash book is required as shown below:

Cash Book									
Date	Details	Discount Allowed	Cash	Bank	Date	Details	Discount Received	Cash	Bank
		£	£	£			£	£	£
1 Jan	Capital			3000.00	1 Jan	Rent			750.00
2 Jan	Sales			330.00	1 Jan	Purchases			950.00
4 Jan	Sales		480.00		1 Jan	Equipment			760.00
5 Jan	Cash (contra)			200.00	5 Jan	Bank (contra)		200.00	
6 Jan	Frank Jones			400.00	5 Jan	Wages		180.00	
					5 Jan	Drawings			500.00
					6 Jan	Apples Galore			500.00
					6 Jan	**Dome & Son**	**2.00**		**48.00**

Dome & Son offer a 4% discount for prompt payment and advantage is taken of this such that only £48.00 is paid for the £50.00 invoice number I2554367. The £2.00 discount received needs to be entered into Dome & Son's account in the sales ledger and into the discount received account in the nominal ledger. Discount allowed would be entered (posted) to the customer's account in the sales ledger and the discount allowed account in the nominal ledger.

Purchase Ledger (from 4.4)

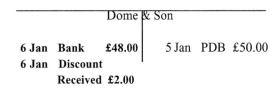

Dome & Son

6 Jan Bank £48.00	5 Jan PDB £50.00
6 Jan Discount	
Received £2.00	

Nominal Ledger

Discount Received	
	6 Jan Dome & Son £2.00

It can be seen from the illustrations above that the double entry will be to two different ledgers as follows:

Sales Day Book – to Sales Ledger and Nominal Ledger

Purchases Day Book – to Purchase Ledger and Nominal Ledger

Sales Returns Day Book – to Sales Ledger and Nominal Ledger

Purchases Returns Day Book – to Purchase Ledger and Nominal Ledger

Cash Receipts - to Cash Book and Nominal Ledger

Cash Payments - to Cash Book and Nominal l Ledger

Petty Cash Receipts - to Petty Cash Book and Nominal Ledger

Petty Cash Payments - to Petty Cash Book and Nominal l Ledger

Supplier Payments - to Cash Book and Purchase Ledger

Customer Receipts – to Cash Book and Sales Ledger

Once all the entries have been made into the ledger accounts it is time to check the accuracy of the information recorded.

Chapter 5 | Trial Balance (Checking Information)

Objectives
By the end of the Chapter you will be able to describe

☐ trial balance

5.1 | Introduction

A trial balance is extracted at the end of an accounting period, which may be weekly, monthly, quarterly or annually. The trial balance consists of two columns, one for debit balances and one for credit balances. The total of each column should be the same i.e. they should balance.

If they balance, it means that the same amounts have been entered on either side of the ledger accounts. The trial balance therefore checks the accuracy of the accounting entries made using the double entry system.

5.2 | Balancing the Accounts

In order to check the accuracy of the information recorded by extracting a trial balance it is first necessary to balance the accounts. To do this the following steps should be taken:

1. Add up the debit and credit side separately to discover which is the larger of the two. Keep a record of these figures but do not enter them anywhere at this stage.

2. Below the last entry on the side which has the most entries draw a line and underneath enter the larger figure calculated above. Then double underline this figure.

3. Also put this figure on the other side but in a parallel position, with a line above and double underline below.

4. Underneath the last entry (but above the line) on the smaller side enter the date on which balancing is to occur e.g. the end of the week or month. Next to the date write "Balance carried down" or "Balance c/d". Subtract the smaller figure from the larger figure calculated in No 1 above and enter this amount next to the "Balance c/d".

5. On the opposite side from the "Balance c/d" but on the line below the double underlining enter the day after the one on which balancing occurred as the date. This time write "Balance brought down" or "Balance b/d" and the monetary amount calculated in No 4.

Illustration 5.1 (from 4.11)

Frank Jones' account in the sales ledger will now be balanced.

Steps

1. Larger side totals (debit side) £500.00, smaller side totals (credit side) £400.00

2.

Sales Ledger

Frank Jones

3 Jan	SDB	£400.00	6 Jan Bank		£400.00
6 Jan	SDB	£100.00			
		£500.00			

3.

Frank Jones

3 Jan	SDB	£400.00	6 Jan Bank		£400.00
6 Jan	SDB	£100.00			
		£500.00			**£500.00**

4.

Frank Jones

3 Jan	SDB	£400.00	6 Jan Bank	£400.00
6 Jan	SDB	£100.00	**7 Jan Balance c/d**	**£100.00**
		£500.00		£500.00

5.

Frank Jones

3 Jan	SDB	£400.00	6 Jan Bank	£400.00
6 Jan	SDB	£100.00	7 Jan Balance c/d	£100.00
		£500.00		£500.00
8 Jan	**Balance b/d**	**£100.00**		

This balance has been calculated by £500.00 - £400.00 = £100.00

The "**Balance c/d**" indicates the amount of money owed to the business i.e. £100.00 by its customer Frank Jones at the **close** of business on 7 January, which is the same as the amount of money owed to the business at the **beginning** of business on 8 January, the "**Balance b/d**".

Entering these balances twice is an application of the principles of double entry.

Thus all accounts need to be balanced using the same principles, so long as there are at least two items entered in the accounts. These can be on the same side, Illustration 5.2 or on opposite sides Illustration 5.3.

Illustration 5.2 (from 4.8)
Nominal Ledger

Purchases

1 Jan Bank	£950.00		
7 Jan PDB	£900.00		

As there are no entries on the credit side, the total is zero and thus the debit side is the larger side £1850.00 and both sides need to add up to this amount.

Purchases

1 Jan Bank	£950.00	7 Jan Balance c/d	£1850.00
7 Jan PDB	£900.00		
	£1850.00		£1850.00
8 Jan Balance b/d	£1850.00		

Illustration 5.3 (from 4.6)
Purchase Ledger

Beautiful Bottles

3 Jan PRDB	£20.00	2 Jan PDB	£200.00
7 Jan Balance c/d	£180.00		
	£200.00		£200.00
		8 Jan Balance b/d	£180.00

The balance b/d can be on either side, as in Illustration 5.2 it is a debit balance, whereas in Illustration 5.3 it is a credit balance.

If there is only a single entry it is not necessary to balance the account as in the case of the capital account reproduced below.

Illustration 5.4 (from 4.7)

Capital

		1 Jan Bank	£3000.00

If the amounts are identical on either side then there will not be a balance on the account at all.

Illustration 5.6 (from 4.12)

Dome & Son

6 Jan Bank	£48.00	5 Jan PDB	£50.00
6 Jan Discount Received	£2.00		
7 Jan Balance c/d	£0.00		
	£50.00		£50.00
		8 Jan Balance b/d	£0.00

Sales Ledger Balances are:

Frank Jones (from 4.11)

3 Jan SDB	£400.00	6 Jan Bank	£400.00
6 Jan SDB	£100.00	7 Jan Balance c/d	£100.00
	£500.00		£500.00
8 Jan Balance b/d	**£100.00**		

James Lloyd (from 4.5)

1 Jan SDB	£315.00	2 Jan SRDB	£15.00
		7 Jan Balance c/d	£300.00
	£315.00		£315.00
8 Jan Balance b/d	**£300.00**		

Wilson Bros (from 4.3)

4 Jan SDB	**£600.00**		

Purchases Ledger Balances are:

Apples Galore (from 4.11)

6 Jan Bank	£500.00	1 Jan PDB	£500.00
7 Jan Balance c/d	£150.00	4 Jan PDB	£150.00
	£650.00		£650.00
		8 Jan Balance b/d	**£150.00**

Beautiful Bottles (from 4.6)

3 Jan	PRDB	£20.00	2 Jan	PDB	£200.00
7 Jan	Balance c/d	£180.00			
		£200.00			£200.00
			8 Jan	**Balance b/d**	**£180.00**

Dome & Son (from 5.6)

6 Jan	Bank	£48.00	5 Jan	PDB	£50.00
6 Jan	Discount Received	£2.00			
7 Jan	Balance c/d	£0.00			
		£50.00			£50.00
			8 Jan	**Balance b/d**	**£0.00**

Nominal Ledger Balances are:

Purchases (from 4.8)

1 Jan	Bank	£950.00	7 Jan	Balance c/d	£1850.00
7 Jan	PDB	£900.00			
		£1850.00			£1850.00
8 Jan	**Balance b/d**	**£1850.00**			

Sales (from 4.8)

7 Jan	Balance c/d	£2225.00	2 Jan	Bank	£330.00
			4 Jan	Cash	£480.00
			7 Jan	SDB	£1415.00
		£2225.00			£2225.00
			8 Jan	**Balance b/d**	**£2225.00**

Sales Returns (from 4.5)

7 Jan SRDB	**£15.00**		

Purchases Returns (from 4.6)

		7 Jan PRDB	**£20.00**

Rent (from 4.7)

1 Jan Bank	**£1250.00**		

Wages (from 4.7)

5 Jan Cash	**£180.00**		

	Equipment (from 4.7)				Discount Received (from 4.12)	

Equipment (from 4.7)

1 Jan Bank	£760.00

Discount Received (from 4.12)

	6 Jan Dome & Son	£2.00

Capital (from 4.9)

7 Jan Balance c/d	£3050.00	1 Jan Bank	£3000.00
		1 Jan Petty Cash	£50.00
	£3050.00		£3050.00
		8 Jan Balance b/d	£3050.00

Petty Cash Book Balances are:

Petty Cash Book (from 4.9)

Receipts £	Date	Details	Voucher No	Total £	Travel £	Stationery £	Postage £	Cleaning £
50.00	1 Jan	Cash Introduced						
	1 Jan	New Petty Cash Book	001	12.50		12.50		
	2 Jan	Postage Stamps	002	7.00			7.00	
	3 Jan	Taxi Fare	003	3.00	3.00			
	5 Jan	Cleaning Materials	004	5.00				5.00
	7 Jan	Envelopes	005	2.50		2.50		
				30.00	3.00	15.00	7.00	5.00
	7 Jan	Balance c/d		20.00				
50.00				50.00				
20.00	7 Jan	Balance b/d						
30.00	7 Jan	Bank						

Although the petty cash payments have been entered into the nominal ledger the imprest amount of £100.00 has yet to be restored. As can be seen above £30.00 has been spent and thus that is the amount needed to refund the imprest. This imprest amount will come from the bank and needs to be entered in the main cash book on the next page.

Cash Book Balances are:

Note the addition of the £30.00 for petty cash.

		Cash Book (from 4.12)								
Date	**Details**	**Discount Allowed**	**Cash £**	**Bank £**	**Date**	**Details**	**Discount Received**	**Cash £**	**Bank £**
1 Jan	Capital			3000.00	1 Jan	Rent			750.00
2 Jan	Sales			330.00	1 Jan	Purchases			950.00
4 Jan	Sales		480.00		1 Jan	Equipment			760.00
5 Jan	Cash (contra)			200.00	5 Jan	Bank (contra)		200.00	
6 Jan	Frank Jones			400.00	5 Jan	Wages		180.00	
					5 Jan	Drawings			500.00
					6 Jan	Apples Galore			500.00
					6 Jan	Dome & Son	2.00		48.00
					7 Jan	Petty Cash			30.00
					7 Jan	Balance c/d		100.00	
			480.00	3930.00				480.00	3930.00
8 Jan	Balance b/d			100.00					

The principle of balancing is exactly the same here, it just needs to be remembered that the cash book is two accounts (cash and bank) contained in one book. Thus each account needs to be balanced separately. As can be seen above the balance of cash is £100.00.

		Cash Book								
Date	**Details**	**Discount Allowed**	**Cash £**	**Bank £**	**Date**	**Details**	**Discount Received**	**Cash £**	**Bank £**
1 Jan	Capital			3000.00	1 Jan	Rent			750.00
2 Jan	Sales			330.00	1 Jan	Purchases			950.00
4 Jan	Sales		480.00		1 Jan	Equipment			760.00
5 Jan	Cash (contra)			200.00	5 Jan	Bank (contra)		200.00	
6 Jan	Frank Jones			400.00	5 Jan	Wages		180.00	
					5 Jan	Drawings			500.00
					6 Jan	Apples Galore			500.00
					6 Jan	Dome & Son	2.00		48.00
					7 Jan	Petty Cash			30.00
					7 Jan	Balance c/d		100.00	**392.00**
			480.00	3930.00				480.00	3930.00
8 Jan	Balance b/d		100.00	**392.00**					

It can now be seen that there is £392.00 in the bank at the end of the week. Care needs to be taken when balancing the bank account as the balance could also be a credit balance b/d which would mean that the account was overdrawn.

The two balances for bank and cash are shown separately on the trial balance.

Extracting the Trial Balance

Once all the accounts have been balanced, their arithmetical accuracy can be checked by extracting a trial balance. This is done by listing all of the accounts from illustration 5.6 and then entering the balance on the account into either a debit or credit column, as appropriate.

Illustration 5.7

A J Dowle

Trial Balance as at 7 January

	Debit £	Credit £
Sales		2225
Purchases	1850	
Sales Returns	15	
Purchases Returns		20
Capital		3050
Rent	1250	
Wages	180	
Equipment	760	
Discount Received		2
Travel	3	
Stationery	15	
Postage	7	
Cleaning	5	
Petty Cash	50	
Cash	100	
Bank	392	
Wilson Bros	600	
Frank Jones	100	
James Lloyd	300	
Beautiful Bottles		180
Apples Galore		150
Dome & Son		nil
	5627	5627

Once all the balances have been entered the columns are totalled. The final figure should be the same in both columns. If this is not the case it means that there is an error which needs to be located by rechecking the additions, the entries into the accounts and onto the trial balance, (called postings) and the balancing.

Errors

Not all errors will prevent a trial balance from balancing. The errors that are not revealed are:

- **Errors of principle** – e.g. purchase cost of a motor vehicle of £10,000 entered as motor expenses. The wrong account and the wrong type of account is used i.e. revenue instead of capital.
- **Errors of commission** - e.g. £130 for Mrs P Jones entered in Mr D Jones' account. The wrong account but the right type of account is used.
- **Total omission** - e.g. a purchase invoice for £410 not entered at all
- **Reversal of entries** – e.g. a debit entry of 110 is put on the credit side and the credit entry of 110 is put on the debit side.

- **Error of original entry** –e.g. a payment for telephone of £120 is entered as a debit in telephone and a credit in cash as£12.
- **Compensating errors** – e.g. the purchases account is entered as £100 too much (debit side) and the capital account is entered as £100 too much (credit side). The errors cancel each other out.

The errors that will stop a trial balance from balancing are :

- **Transposition errors** – e.g. a balance entered as £150 instead of as £105
- **One sided omission** – e.g. a credit entry made of £200 in the cash book but no debit entry made in the creditor's account
- **Both entries on the same side** –e.g. a cash sale of £325 entered as a credit in the cash account and as a credit in the sales account. (NB you need to double the amount to correct this error)
- **A balance omitted** – e.g. a balance of £535 on telephone not entered in the trial balance.
- **A balance entered on the wrong side** - e.g. discount received of £85 entered on the debit side instead of the credit side.
- **Account totalled incorrectly** - e.g.sales undercast (too little) by £320

5.5 | Suspense Account

If the errors prevent the trial balance from balancing, it is temporarily balanced by the use of a suspense account whilst the discrepancy is investigated. Thus the difference between the credit side and the debit side is entered into the suspense account on the appropriate side to make the trial balance agree.

Illustration 5.8

A J Dowle

Trial Balance as at 7 January

	Debit £	Credit £
Sales		2215
Purchases	1850	
Sales Returns	15	
Purchases Returns		20
Capital		3050
Rent	1250	
Wages	180	
Equipment	670	
Discount Received	2	
Travel	3	
Stationery	15	
Postage	7	
Cleaning	5	
Petty Cash	50	
Cash	100	
Bank	392	
Wilson Bros	600	
Frank Jones	100	
James Lloyd	300	
Beautiful Bottles		180
Apples Galore		nil
Dome & Son		150
Suspense	**76**	
	5615	**5615**

The trial balance in Illustration 5.7 has been altered so that it no longer balances.
A suspense account has been created with a debit balance of £76 as the debit side of the trial balance only totalled £5539 not £5615

5.6   Journals

Although a suspense account has been created it must not remain and thus the errors need to be discovered and amended. This is done by means of journal entries, as these are used to record the double entry necessary to correct the errors. Each journal entry should have:

- the date
- the name of the account to be debited and the amount
- the name of the account to be credited and the amount
- a narrative - a description of the transaction
- underlining

Date year	Details	Debit £	Credit £
xxx	Account to be debited	X	
	Account to be credited		X
	Narrative –being the……..		

At present the suspense account has a balance of £76.00 on the debit side as shown below:

Suspense

7 Jan Per Trial Balance	£76	

This difference is investigated and the following errors come to light:

- Discount received of £2.00 has been recorded as a debit entry in the discount received account. The entry in the supplier's account has been correctly made.

- The credit side of the sales account has been undercast by £10.00

- The payment for equipment of £760 has been entered in the equipment account as £670

- The balance of £150 on Apples Galore account has been credited to Dome & Son's account in error.

These errors will be corrected by the use of journal entries. This will be done by the appropriate entry, debit or credit being made in the relevant account and the opposite entry being made in the suspense account. The necessary journal entries are:

Date	Details	Debit £	Credit £
7 Jan	Suspense	4.00	
	Discount Received		4.00

Being the correction of a misposting of the balance on the discount received account of £2.00 to the debit side instead of the credit side.

(Remember as the amount is on the wrong side it needs to be doubled to correct the error i.e. once to take the wrong entry out and once to put the correct entry in)

Date	Details	Debit £	Credit £
7 J an	Suspense	10.00	
	Sales		10.00

Being the correction of the undercast on the sales account

Date	Details	Debit £	Credit £
7 Jan	Equipment	90.00	
	Suspense		90.00

Being the correction of a transposition error where the equipment was debited as £670.00 instead of £760.00. (760-670=90)

Date	Details	Debit £	Credit £
7 Jan	Dome & Son	150.00	
	Apples Galore		150.00

Being the correction of an error of commission where the credit balance was put to the wrong account.

The suspense account will now be cleared as follows:

Suspense

7 Jan	Per Trial Balance	£76	7 Jan	Equipment	£90
7 Jan	Discount Received	£4			
7 Jan	Sales	£10			
		£90			£90

Notice that the error of commission did not prevent the trial balance from balancing and thus is not entered in the suspense account.

Chapter 6 — Final Accounts (Presenting Information)

Objectives
By the end of the Chapter you will be able to describe

☐ final accounts

6.1 Introduction

The trial balance is used to prepare the final accounts of the business, which consist of a trading account, a profit and loss account and a balance sheet. They enable the business to assess how successful it has been in terms of gross profit, in the trading account and net profit in the profit and loss account. Expenses and revenues are therefore found in the trading and profit and loss accounts whereas the balance sheet on the other hand shows the assets, capital and liabilities of the business.

6.2 Balance Sheet

Balance sheets are 'snapshots' of a business on a particular date. This is the last day of the accounting period, which is usually a date at the end of a calendar month e.g. 31 December. Accounting periods are normally for one year. Thus a balance sheet would be drawn up on the 31 December each year to show the assets, liabilities and capital of the business on that particular date.

A **balance sheet** is divided into two halves, usually showing net assets i.e. assets less liabilities in the top half and capital in the bottom half. It shows the assets used by the business and how they have been financed. An illustration is provided below:

Illustration 6.1

Name of Business
Balance Sheet as at (date)

	£
Assets	X
Less Liabilities	(X)
Net Assets	X
Capital	X

In other words assets minus liabilities equals capital. Thus the total value in the top half of the balance sheet will equal the total value in the bottom half **i.e. balance!**

This is the Accounting Equation A – L = C (assets minus liabilities equals capital)

Assets are resources owned by the business. They are **debit** balances on the trial balance. Assets in the balance sheet are divided into **fixed assets** and **current assets**.

Fixed assets are items owned by a business, which it expects to keep for some years i.e. they are long term assets. They are bought to enable the business to trade. Thus they are to be used in the business (rather than sold to a customer). They represent capital expenditure, which is expenditure on the purchase (including delivery and installation), alteration or improvement of fixed assets. Examples are:

- Land
- Buildings
- Machinery
- Equipment
- Motor Vehicles
- Fixtures and Fittings

Current assets are owned by the business where the value is constantly changing i.e. they are short term assets. They may either be items owned by the business with the intention of turning them into cash within one year or actual cash, including money in the business bank account. Examples are:

- Stocks
- Debtors (people who owe the business money i.e. customers)
- Cash at Bank
- Cash in Hand

Liabilities are amounts owed by the business. Liabilities in the balance sheet are divided into **long term liabilities** and **current liabilities**. They are credit balances on the trial balance.

Long Term Liabilities are amounts owed by the business which will not be repaid for at least one year. Often the liabilities will be for a much longer period of time e.g. a mortgage for 25 years. Examples are:

- Loans
- Mortgages

Current Liabilities are amounts owed by the business whose value changes on a regular basis i.e. they are short term liabilities. Examples are:

- Creditors (people who the business owes money i.e. suppliers
- Bank overdraft

Capital is the total of the resources supplied to a business by the owner. Therefore it is owed back to the owner by the business. It is a **credit** balance on the trial balance. The owner will probably take cash or goods out of the business for his private use. These amounts are known as **drawings** and are deducted from the capital amount. It is a **debit** balance on the trial balance.

Thus the balance sheet can be expanded as follows:

Illustration 6.2

Name of Business
Balance Sheet as at (date)

	£	£
Fixed Assets		
Fixed Asset A		X
Current Assets		
Closing Stock	X	
Debtors	X	
Cash at Bank	X	
Cash in Hand	X	
	X	
Less Current Liabilities		
Creditors	(X)	
		X
Net Assets		X
Financed by		
Capital		X
Add Net Profit		X
		X
Less Drawings		(X)
Closing Capital		X

The left hand column is the working column and is used for calculations, which are transferred to the right hand column.

Once a single line is drawn it means that the figures above are either going to be added together or subtracted from each other. A bracket round an (X) means that the figures are to be subtracted e.g. current liabilities are subtracted from current assets.

6.3 Trading Accounts and Profit and Loss Accounts

Trading Accounts and Profit And Loss Accounts are statements that match the revenue earned in a period with the expenses incurred in earning it. They show whether the revenue is greater than the expenses i.e. the business has made a profit or, whether the expenses are greater than the revenue i.e. the business has made a loss.

Revenue is the income received by selling the goods of the business. It is usually called **sales** or turnover of the business and is a **credit** balance in the trial balance. The goods bought by the business for the purposes of resale are called **purchases** and are **debit** balances in the trial balance. Expenses are the costs of operating the business and are **debit** balances in the trial balance

The trading and profit and loss account shows the revenue and expenses for an accounting period, usually for a twelve month period ending on the day that the balance sheet is prepared. If the trading and profit and loss account was for the year ended 31 December, it would cover the revenue received and the expenses incurred from the 1 January to the 31 December.

6.4 Trading Account

The **trading account** calculates the **gross profit**, which is the difference between the sales revenue received and the cost of the goods sold in the period.

- Sales minus Cost of Sales = Gross Profit

Illustration 6.3

Name of Business
Trading Account for the year ended (date)

	£
Sales	X
Less Cost of Sales	(X)
Gross Profit	**X**

The cost of the goods sold represents the actual goods, which have been sold as opposed to the purchases that have been made. There is a difference because some of the goods purchased during the year will not be sold; they are still in stock. For example if 100 items were purchased during the year ended 31 December but only 80 items were sold there would still be 20 items in stock at the year end (31 December) i.e. purchases less closing stock equals cost of sales.

If the business has been trading for more than a year it may have some stock left from last year, this now becomes opening stock for the current year. In the example above, the 20 items of closing stock at the end of the accounting period 31 December would be opening stock on 1 January in the following year. If 200 items were purchased during the following year and there were 30 items unsold; the amount of goods sold would be the original 20, plus the 200 minus the 30, which equals 190. In other words:

- Opening Stock plus Purchases minus Closing Stock = Cost of Sales

Illustration 6.4

Name of Business
Trading Account for the year ended (date)

	£	£
Sales		X
Less Cost of Sales		
Opening Stock	X	
Add Purchases	X	
	X	
Less Closing Stock	(X)	
		(X)*
Gross Profit		**X**

* = This is the total cost of sales (or goods sold)

At the end of the year stock should be professionally valued. It is important that the figure is accurate as it effects gross profit as if it is overstated it will increase gross profit, whereas a figure for closing stock that is understated will reduce gross profit.

6.5   Profit and Loss Account

The **profit and loss account** calculates the **net profit**, which is what is left after the expenses of running the business have been deducted from the gross profit.

- Gross Profit minus Expenses = Net Profit

Illustration 6.4

Name of Business
Profit and Loss Account for the year ended (date)

	£
Gross Profit	X
Less Expenses	(X)
Net Profit	X

There are many different expenses of running a business and they vary according to the type of business. However, they all represent revenue expenditure, which means that they are day-to-day costs of the business, either selling, distribution or administrative. They include the costs of maintaining and repairing fixed assets. All revenue expenditure is shown in the profit and loss account and reduces the ultimate profit figure.

Illustration 6.5

Name of Business
Profit and Loss Account for the year ended (date)

	£	£
Gross Profit		X
Less Expenses		
Expense A	X	
Expense B	X	
Expense C	X	
Expense D	X	
		(X)
Net Profit		X

The (X) means these figures are to be deducted from the figures above.

The expenses are labelled A-D as it is not known in advance what they are or how many there will be. Examples are wages and salaries, rent, electricity and general expenses.

Advanced Trading and Profit and Loss Account

Often the trading and profit and loss account is called a profit and loss account for short but it is actually two accounts, being the trading account and the profit and loss account joined into one. It is usually shown however all as one account rather than two separate accounts.

The trading account described above is a basic account that does not include the following:

- Sales returns
- Purchases returns
- Carriage inwards – the delivery costs of buying goods from suppliers

Like the trading account, there are other items which could be included in a profit and loss account. These are:

- Discount received
- Discount allowed
- Carriage outwards - the delivery costs of selling goods to customers

These should be incorporated into the trading and profit and loss account as follows:

Illustration 6.6

Name of Business
Trading and Profit and Loss Account for the year ended (date)

	£	£
Sales		X
Less Sales Returns		(X)
		X
Less Cost of Sales		
Opening Stock	X	
Add Purchases	X	
Add Carriage Inwards	X	
Less Purchase Returns	(X)	
	X	
Less Closing Stock	(X)	
		(X)
Gross Profit		X
Add Discount Received		X
		X
Less Expenses		
Expense A	X	
Expense B	X	
Expense C	X	
Expense D	X	
Carriage Outwards	X	
Discount Allowed	X	
		(X)
Net Profit		X

The trial balance from illustration 5.7 has been reproduced below:

A J Dowle
Trial Balance as at 7 January

	Debit £	Credit £
Sales		2225
Purchases	1850	
Sales Returns	15	
Purchases Returns		20
Capital		3050
Rent	1250	
Wages	180	
Equipment	760	
Discount Received		2
Travel	3	
Stationery	15	
Postage	7	
Cleaning	5	
Petty Cash	50	
Cash	100	
Bank	392	
Wilson Bros	600	
Frank Jones	100	
James Lloyd	300	
Beautiful Bottles		180
Apples Galore		150
Dome & Son		nil
	5627	5627

Illustration 6.8

The trading and profit and loss account can now be prepared but there is one piece of information missing. This is the value of closing stock at 7 January, which is £735.

A J Dowle
Trading and Profit and Loss Account for the period ended 7 January

	£	£
Sales		2225.00
Less Sales Returns		(15.00)
		2210.00
Less Cost of Sales		
Opening Stock	Nil	
Add Purchases	1850.00	
Add Carriage Inwards	Nil	
Less Purchase Returns	(20.00)	
	1830.00	
Less Closing Stock	(735.00)	
		(1095.00)
Gross Profit		**1115.00**
Add Discount Received		2.00
		1117.00
Less Expenses		
Rent	750.00	
Wages	180.00	
Travel	3.00	
Stationery	15.00	
Postage	7.00	
Cleaning	5.00	
Carriage Outwards	nil	
Discount Allowed	nil	
		(960.00)
Net Profit		**157.00**

The headings that are nil have been included for completeness but in reality would be excluded. As this is the first year of the business there is no opening stock.

A J Dowle
Balance Sheet as at 7 January

	£	£
Fixed Assets		
Equipment		760.00
Current Assets		
Closing Stock	735.00	
Debtors	1000.00	
Cash at Bank	392.00	
Cash in Hand	* 150.00	
	2277.00	
Less Current Liabilities		
Creditors	(330.00)	
		1947.00
Net Assets		**2707.00**
Financed by		
Capital		3050.00
Add Net Profit		157.00
		3207.00
Less Drawings		(500.00)
Closing Capital		**2707.00**

* The cash figure of £100.00 and the petty cash figure of £50.00 have been added together. In reality it is unlikely that a business would have both figures as they would either have petty cash in a tin or have a cash float in a till but it is possible.

6.6   Adjustments

There is however a number of adjustments, which need be made to the final accounts at the year end in order to show a more realistic view of the state of the business. Final accounts are prepared on the income and expenditure basis rather than the receipts and payments basis. This means that they should reflect the revenue that has been earned and the costs that have been incurred for the year and not the amounts that has been received or paid.

These adjustments are:

- Accruals
- Prepayments
- Depreciation
- Bad Debts
- Doubtful Debts
- Goods for Own Use

Accruals

An accrual is an amount due in an accounting period, which is unpaid at the end of that period e.g. electricity bill accrued (i.e. owing). It is:

- added to the expense e.g. electricity in the trial balance before listing it in the profit and loss account (debit)
- shown as a current liability called accruals in the year-end balance sheet. (credit)

Prepayments

A prepayment is a payment made in advance of the accounting period to which it relates e.g. rent prepaid (i.e. in advance). It is:

- deducted from the appropriate expense e.g. rent in the trial balance before listing it in the profit and loss account (credit)
- shown as a current asset called prepayments in the year-end balance sheet. (debit)

Depreciation

Depreciation is the part of the cost of a fixed asset that is consumed during its period of use by the business. Fixed assets lose value over time as a result of being used by the business i.e. they wear out. This loss in value has to be calculated and recorded in the accounts.

Depreciation may be calculated by using the straight line method or the reducing (diminishing) balance method. The **straight line method** calculates depreciation at an equal amount each year **based on the cost** of the asset. With the **reducing balance method** a fixed percentage **based on the net value** of the asset (cost less depreciation to date i.e. provision for depreciation) is deducted, which provides a depreciation charge that is smaller each time it is calculated. Regardless of which method is used it is:

- shown as an expense called depreciation in the profit and loss account (debit)
- shown as a(1st year)/ or added to the (subsequent years) provision for depreciation account (credit) and then
- deducted from the value of the asset in the balance sheet

Illustration 6.9

If an asset was purchased for £10000 and had a life of five years, the depreciation charge would be £2000 per annum (£10000 divided by 5) using the straight line method. The same asset of £10000 depreciated at 20% per annum using the reducing balance method would be as follows:

Cost	£10000
less 20%	**£2000**
Value at	
End year 1	£8000
less 20%	**£1600**
Value at	
End year 2	£6400
less 20%	**£1280**
Value at	
End year 3	**£5120**

This process would carry on until the asset had been fully depreciated or sold.

The depreciation appears in both the profit and loss account and the balance sheet. The charge for the year is included as an expense in the profit and loss account and as a reduction in the value of the fixed assets in the balance sheet.

Bad Debts

Most businesses when selling goods to other businesses do not receive payment immediately, as they sell on credit and therefore have debtors. Unfortunately not all debtors eventually pay and thus they become bad debts. This means that the business gives up trying to collect the debt, thereby closing the debtor's account and accepting the loss.

The amount owing is:
- shown as an expense called bad debt written off in the profit and loss account (debit)
- deducted from the debtors figure prior to inclusion in current assets in the balance sheet (credit)

Illustration 6.10

If the total debtors figure was £3123, and the debtor who owed £123 was unable to pay, the following would take place:

- there would be an expense called bad debt written off of £123 in the profit and loss account (this would reduce profit)
- the £123 would be deducted from the £3123 and the £3000 would be shown in current assets in the balance sheet

Doubtful Debts

As well as debts which have gone bad, businesses may have concerns over the ability of debtors to pay. On the basis of past experience they are able to estimate what percentage of total debtors this may be applicable to e.g. 2% and set up a provision for doubtful debts (also called provision for bad debts). The amount of the provision is:

- shown as an expense called provision for doubtful debts in the profit and loss account (debit)
- entered into a provision for doubtful debts account(credit) and show it on the balance sheet as a deduction from the debtors figure in current assets

Goods for Own Use

Goods in which a business trades e.g. a convenience store's producrs may be taken by the owner for his own use. If this occurs:
- add the amount to drawings (debit)
- deduct the amount from purchases (credit)

Illustration 6.10

The trial balance from illustration 5.7 and 6.6 has been reproduced below:

A J Dowle
Trial Balance as at 7 January

	Debit £	Credit £
Sales		2225
Purchases	1850	
Sales Returns	15	
Purchases Returns		20
Capital		3050
Rent	1250	
Wages	180	
Equipment	760	
Discount Received		2
Travel	3	
Stationery	15	
Postage	7	
Cleaning	5	
Petty Cash	50	
Cash	100	
Bank	392	
Wilson Bros	600	
Frank Jones	100	
James Lloyd	300	
Beautiful Bottles		180
Apples Galore		150
Dome & Son		nil
	5627	5627

The following adjustments need to be made:

1. Wages owing £50
2. Rent prepaid £250
3. Depreciation of equipment is at 10 % using the straight line method
4. Create a provision for doubtful debts of 4% of debtors
5. The owner has taken goods for own use of £100

Wages owing £50
Increase wages from £180 to £230 – profit and loss account
Add an accrual of £50 to current liabilities – balance sheet

Rent prepaid £250
Reduce rent from £750 to £600 – profit and loss account
Add a prepayment of £150 to current assets – balance sheet

Depreciation of equipment is at 10 % using the straight line method
Add expense of depreciation for £76.00 (cost of £760.00 x 10%)- profit and loss account
Add provision for depreciation £76.00 - balance sheet

Provision for doubtful debts of 4%
Add expense of provision for doubtful debts of £40 (Debtors of £1000 x 4%) - profit and loss account
Deduct provision for doubtful debts of £40 from debtors – balance sheet

Goods for own use of £100
Reduce purchases from £1850.00 to£1750.00 - profit and loss account
Increase drawings from £500.00 to £600.00 - balance sheet

A J Dowle
Trading and Profit and Loss Account for the period ended 7 January

	£	£
Sales		2225.00
Less Sales Returns		(15.00)
		2210.00
Less Cost of Sales		
Opening Stock	Nil	
Add Purchases (1850.00-100.00)	**1750.00**	
Add Carriage Inwards	Nil	
Less Purchase Returns	(20.00)	
	1730.00	
Less Closing Stock	(735.00)	
		(995.00)
Gross Profit		1215.00
Add Discount Received		2.00
		1217.00
Less Expenses		
Rent (750.00 -150.00)	**600.00**	
Wages (180.00 + 50.00)	**230.00**	
Travel	3.00	
Stationery	15.00	
Postage	7.00	
Cleaning	5.00	
Depreciation	**76.00**	
Provision for Doubtful Debts	**40.00**	
Carriage Outwards	nil	
Discount Allowed	nil	
		(976.00)
Net Profit		**241.00**

A J Dowle
Balance Sheet as at 7 January

			£
Fixed Assets			
Equipment			760.00
Less Provision for Depreciation			**(76.00)**
			684.00
Current Assets			
Closing Stock		735.00	
Debtors	1000.00		
Less Provision for Doubtful Debts	**(40.00)**		
		960.00	
Prepayment		**150.00**	
Cash at Bank		392.00	
Cash in Hand		150.00	
		2387.00	
Current Liabilities			
Creditors	(330.00)		
Accruals	**(50.00)**		
		(380.00)	
			2007.00
Net Assets			2691.00
Capital			3050.00
Add Net Profit			241.00
			3291.00
Less Drawings (500.00 + 100.00)			**(600.00)**
			2691.00

Chapter 7 | Computerised Accounts

Objectives
By the end of the Chapter you will be
able to describe

☐ computerised accounts

7.1 | Introduction

As outlined at the beginning of this book the fundamental principles of bookkeeping are the same whatever method is used to communicate the information, be it manual or computerised. Thus up to this point the accounting system has been described and explained from inception to completion.

7.2 | Differences

However, using a computer does make a difference as there is less for the bookkeeping clerk to do. The clerk only needs to enter the data into the day books, along with the appropriate nominal codes as the computer automatically performs the double entry transactions. In addition the computer carries out these entries much faster than could be achieved manually, not to mention more accurately.

The trial balance and the final accounts are updated after every transaction takes place rather than being extracted when required. This means that they can be produced immediately.

There is no longer a need to total figures and crosscast them as once more this is done automatically on an on-going basis.

7.3 | Errors

As explained in chapter 5 (5.4) there are two types of errors, those that stop a trial balance from balancing and those that do not. Errors that stop a trial balance from balancing **will not** occur with a computerised system as they are all caused by human error. The other errors, that do not stop a trial balance from balancing can and will take place with a computerised system.

7.4 | Corrections

Corrections can be made to any accounting system, be it computerised or manual. It is important that any changes made can be traced i.e. there is an audit trail. Ideally in a manual system compensating entries should be made or a neat horizontal line drawn through the inaccurate item, rather than being painted out with correction fluid. With a computerised system it is also possible to correct errors but any changes made will be recorded, often in red, so that the audit trail is maintained.

7.5 | V.A.T.

V.A.T. stands for value added tax and is added to taxable supplies by registered businesses. Bookkeeping and Accounts Level 1 and Level 2 do not include V.A.T. within their syllabus but Computerised Accounts Level 1 and 2 do.

Most computerised accounts packages default to the standard rate of V.A.T. and calculated the amount automatically. Care needs to be taken to ensure that the amount shown on the invoice or batch control is the same as the amount calculated as this may differ, often by a penny. The figure used should be that taken from the original documentation and thus the amount on screen will need to be altered to agree.

Also when there is no V.A.T on the item the tax code will need to be changed.

7.6 | Computerised Accounts Level 1 and 2

City and Guilds (formerly Pitmans) Computerised Accounts Level 1 and 2 qualification is a generic one and thus a wide variety of accounting software packages may be used. However, the instructions that follow are based on the use of SAGE, a popular accounting package.

7.7 | Computerised Accounts Level 1

With this paper, a specialist teacher is required to input some initial information into the accounting system prior to the start of the examination. The candidate is then required to carry out various tasks. They usually consist of the following:

- Add accounts to the Sales and Purchase Ledger
- Create accounts in the Nominal Ledger
- Update the Sales and Purchase Ledger with invoices
- Enter credit notes into Sales or Purchase Ledger
- Enter receipts in the Sales Ledger
- Enter payments in the Purchase Ledger
- Printout Sales and Purchase Ledger Report(s)
- Printout a Trial Balance

Prior to starting it is advisable to change the program date from its default of today's date, which can be seen in the status bat in the bottom right hand corner of the screen. This will be displayed in the format of date, month and year. Next to this can be seen the month as a word together with the year. This represents the commencement of the financial year for the business.

Click on **Settings** from the main menu bar at the top of the screen and choose **Change Program Date** from the drop down list. Look at the exam paper to find out which month's transactions are to be processed. Enter the last day of this month together with the relevant year, discovered above, in the **Change Program Date** box.

7.7.1 Computerised Accounts Level 1

Select the **Customers** icon on the tool bar in the main option window and the sub option window will be displayed. Select **Record** to add accounts. At the opening of the screen the cursor will be flashing in the box called **A/C**. Enter the appropriate code.

Click at the beginning of the **Name** box and enter their name followed by their full address. Enter these details exactly as shown on the question paper.

Next choose the **Credit Control** tab and click in the **Terms agreed** box in the bottom left hand corner under **Restrictions.** Then click on the **Save** button and enter the next account in the same way.

When all the accounts have been entered, click on **Close** for the sub option window and **Close** again to return to the main option window.

Repeat the process above but this time, select the **Suppliers** icon to add accounts to the Purchase Ledger.

7.7.2 Create Accounts in the Nominal Ledger

Click on **Nominal** and the Nominal Ledger sub option window will be displayed, showing all the nominal accounts and their codes which have already been created. If they are not visable, go to the far right of the screen to the layout box and choose **List** using the drop-down arrow.

Select **Record**, type in the required code next to the flashing cursor in the box called **N/C** and tab. One of two things will happen. Either an account name will be displayed in the **Name** box or it will be blank and **New Account** will appear next to the A/C box. Either way, the identical name shown on the question paper needs to be entered in the **Name** box. Then **Save** and repeat process until all accounts have been created. Choose **Close** to return to the main option window.

7.7.3 | Update the Sales and Purchase Ledger with Invoices

Choose **Customers** again and then **Invoice** from the sub option window. The **Batch Customer Invoices** window will appear. Enter the appropriate details from the Batch Control in the exam paper. Firstly use the drop down arrow in the **A/C** box to enter the account name. The customer's name, the default nominal code name and number for sales (4000), the default tax rate and program date will all be displayed automatically.

Change the date to the one required. Enter the invoice number under **Ref** and ignore Ex Ref and Dept. Check that the default code is the one needed, if not alter as necessary. Under details enter the type of sales e.g. plants shown in the **N/C Name** box. Enter the net amount of the goods and tab, which will cause the default standard rate of V.A.T. to be shown. As explained earlier, check that this is correct, if not change to the right amount. Then enter the next invoice.

When all the invoices have been inputted, enter the Check List Totals fom the Net VAT and Totals boxesonto the exam paper. Once this has been carried out, click on **Save, Close** and **Close** again to return to the main option window.

Now choose **Suppliers** and enter the invoices into the **Purchase Ledger** in the same way as described above. Once again take care to enter the correct nominal codes and the right amount of V.A.T.

7.7.4 | Enter Credit Notes into Sales or Purchase Ledger

From the main option window click on **Customers** or **Suppliers**, depending on whether the credit note is issued or received. For either option, then choose **Credit**. The sub option window is identical to that displayed for invoices except that the coloured sections are red instead of blue.

Enter the required A/C number and the other information provided in the paper. Click on **Save, Close** and **Close** again to return to the main option window.

7.7.5 | Enter Receipts in the Sales Ledger

In order to enter receipts, click on **Bank** and the **Bank Accounts** window will be displayed, with the default bank account 1200 being highlighted in the list box.

As cheques have been received from debtors they need to be entered into the Sales Ledger, therefore **Customer** (not Receipts) needs to be selected from this sub option window.

Enter the A/C number of the customer whose money has been received. The name of the customer, program date and all outstanding invoices will appear. Enter the relevant date, the number of the cheque under reference and at amount, the value of the cheque received.

Next enter the amount received in the receipts column next to the outstanding invoice and tab. Click on **Save, Close** and **Close** again to return to the main option window.

7.7.6 | Enter Payments in the Purchase Ledger

As with receipts, cheque payments to creditors are entered into the Purchase Ledger by first choosing **Bank**, and then **Supplier** from the **Bank Accounts** window.

The sub option window called **Supplier Payment-Bank Current Account** displayed is similar to customer receipt but is made to resemble a cheque.

Enter the reference of the supplier to be paid, the date, the cheque number and the total amount of the cheque in figures. Once Tab has been pressed, the amount in words is entered automatically on the cheque.

The amount paid needs to be entered in the payments column next to the outstanding invoice.

Take care because if this step is omitted and **Save** clicked, a **Confirm** box regarding payments on account will appear. Choose **No** and it will be removed so that the amount paid can be allocated to the invoice.

Now click on **Save, Close** and **Close** again to return to the main option window.

7.7.7 | Printout Sales and Purchase Ledger Report(s)

The Sales and Purchase Ledger Report(s) are to include customer/supplier name, address, account reference number, each transaction and account balance. To obtain this information two different reports need to be printed.

To display the available Sales Ledger Reports, click on **Customers** and then **Reports** from the sub option window. The reports required are Customer Address List and Customer Activity (Summary). Depending on the version of Sage being used, these will either be listed in alphabetical order or can be found under Customer Details Reports and Customer Activity Reports.

Once **Customer Address List** has been located, highlight it and select **Preview** and **Run** or **Generate Report**. Click **OK** when the Criteria box appears and the report will be displayed. Check the details are correct, click on **Print** and choose **OK** from the Print box and **Close**.

Now repeat the process for the **Customer Activity (Summary)** in order to obtain the transactions on the account.

Purchase Ledger Report(s) are identical and obtained in the same way but this time click on **Suppliers** and then **Reports** to access the **Supplier Address List** and **Supplier Activity (Summary)**.

7.7.8 | Printout a Trial Balance

Select **Financials** from the main option window and then click on **Trial** from the Financials window and. Ensure Preview is selected in the Print Output window and choose Run. A Criteria box will appear which should have displayed, by default, the appropriate month and year. If it does not, use the drop down list to choose the right month.

Click on **OK** and the Period Trial Balance can be seen. Choose **Print** and choose **OK** from the Print box. Finally select **Close** and **Close** again to return to the main option window.

The examination is now complete.

7.8 Computerised Accounts Level 2

Prior to commencement of the examination a specialist teacher will have initialised the system but unlike level 1 no initial data e.g. customer account details or invoices will have been inputted. The candidate is usually required to use the documents provided to update the accounts as follows

1. Create accounts for
    Customers
    Sales
    Suppliers
    Purchases
    Nominal

2. Introduce initial capital

3. Enter Purchase Ledger transactions

4. Enter Sales Ledger transactions

5. Enter credit notes into Sales or Purchase Ledger

6. Enter receipts in the Sales Ledger

7. Enter payments in the Purchase Ledger

8. Enter cash payments

9. Enter cash receipts

10. Obtain printouts for
    Sales Ledger Report(s)
    Purchase Ledger Report(s)
    Bank or Cash Account Analysis
    Trial Balance

N.B. Several of the tasks in Level 2 are identical to Level 1. Where this is the case the reader will be referred back to the appropriate section above.

Start by changing the program date to that required by the business in the exam paper (see 7.7)

7.8.1 Create Accounts

Accounts need to be set up for Customers and Suppliers in the Sales and Purchase Ledger (see 7.7.1), as well as for Sales, Purchase and Nominal in the Nominal Ledger (see 7.7.2).

7.8.2 Introduce Initial Capital

Capital is normally introduced into both the Bank Account and the Cash Account at the commencement of the business.

Choose **Bank** from the main option window and the various bank accounts (including cash) will be displayed in the list box. Select **Receipt** and the default bank account name and number (1200), the default tax rate and program date will all be displayed automatically in the **Bank Receipts** window.

Enter the right date, the reference supplied and the nominal code for capital (usually 3000) as well as capital introduced under details. In the net column put the total amount of money paid into the bank account and tab. The accounting system will automatically calculate V.A.T on this amount, therefore the T1 in the T/C column needs to be changed to T9 (this is the code for transactions not involving VAT). This will change the tax column to zero. Tab back to the start.

In order to enter the cash use the drop down arrow in the bank column to select 1230 the default code for cash. When this is entered the name in the box next to Bank at the top of the screen will be Cash. Enter the other details remembering to change the tax code to T9. Check that the amount shown in the Total box in the top right hand side of the screen is correct and then click **Save, Close** and **Close** again to return to the main option window.

7.8.3 Enter Purchase and Sales Ledger Transactions

In the exam paper there will be a detachable sheet that is double sided with Purchase Batch Control on one side and Sales Batch Control on the other. There will also be several purchase and sales invoices on the exam paper. The relevant information needs to be extracted from them and entered manually onto the appropriate Batch Control.

Care needs to be taken when entering the information to ensure that the correct date is used i.e. the invoice date and not the order date.

Particular attention needs to be paid to the account number when entering the purchase invoices as the number required is the account number given to the supplier in 7.8.1 above and **not** the account number on the invoice.

When there is more than one item on an invoice these need to be entered separately as they will have different nominal codes.

Once all the amounts have been entered onto the Batch Totals the individual columns should be added up and cross cast.

The instructions on the exam paper say that the Batch Control should be used to enter the data into the computer; however more able students also use the exam paper so that they can enter the quantities as well. To update the Sales and Purchase Ledger with the invoices see 7.7.3, however before the data is saved ensure that the manual Check List Totals agree with the Net, VAT and Total boxes on screen.

7.8.4 Enter Credit Notes into Sales or Purchase Ledger Transactions - see 7.7.4 above

The only difference is the nominal account code will not be given but the goods need to be credited back to the account code used when they were sold or purchased originally.

7.8.5 Enter Receipts in the Sales Ledger - see 7.7.5 above

Care needs to be taken with these receipts when the cheque received is allocated as it is probable that there will be more than one outstanding invoice. Thus one cheque may pay one or more invoices.

7.8.6 Enter Payments in the Purchase Ledger - see 7.7.6 above

As in 7.7.5 above they may be more than one invoice unpaid and the payment made may be for two invoices or only a part payment of an invoice.

It may occur that the payment is the balance outstanding after a credit note has been received e.g. £60.00. In this case, the amount of the credit note, £5.80 needs to be entered in the payment column first and then the total amount of the invoice, £65.80. The system will deduct the credit note from the invoice to get to the amount of the payment £60.00. This will be displayed in the analysis box (bottom right of the screen).

7.8.7 Enter Cash Receipts

As explained in 7.8.2, it is necessary to select **Bank** and then **Receipt** to enter cash receipts. This is because cash is regarded as a type of bank account. The important thing to remember is that the code needs to be changed at the Bank Receipt window to 1230 for Cash.

The exam paper will provide the details needed with regard to date and reference but not nominal code. As with the credit note (see 7.8.4 above) the narrative given as to the goods sold will enable the correct nominal code to be found. This can be done either by looking back in the exam paper to the nominal codes entered originally, or by clicking on the drop down arrow in the **N/C** box and scrolling through the list.

Just as capital introduced has no tax, the details provided may say that there is no tax on this amount. In this case the tax code needs to be changed from T1 to T9 (see 7.8.2)

Another matter relating to tax is where a total figure is given and then it says that this amount includes tax e.g. total amount £258.50, including tax of £38.50. This means that the net amount is in fact £220.00. If this is the case enter the total figure in the net column i.e. £258.50 and click on the **Calc Net** button in the bottom left hand corner of the screen. The system will change the net figure to the right amount £220.00 and enter the accurate tax, £38.50 in the tax column.

7.8.8 | Enter Cash Payments

This is identical to entering cash receipts, including the screen, only that after **Bank** choose **Payment**. Also quite naturally the sub option window is called Bank Payment and unlike the Supplier Payment does not resemble a cheque.

Just as with cash receipts (7.8.7 above) the nominal code will not be given and there may be no tax or payments will include the tax.

7.8.9 | Obtain Printouts - see 7.7.7 and 7.7.8 above

The printouts for Sales Ledger Report(s) and Purchase Ledger Report(s) are produced in exactly the same way as for Level 1 except that the Customer/Supplier Activity Report is Customer/Supplier Activity (Detailed) not (Summary).

The Trial Balance is also identical.

There is however an additional report which is required. This is usually the Bank Account Analysis but may be the Cash Account Analysis.

Select **Nominal** (note not Bank) from the main option window and then highlight **1200 Bank Current Account** or **1230 Cash** in the list box, depending on which report is required. If it is not displayed, select List from the Layout box on the right of the screen. It is **very** important this is done as otherwise there is a danger that all nominal accounts will be printed.

Now click on the **Reports** icon and choose **Nominal Activity**. If not shown, click on **Nominal Activity Reports**. Ensure **Preview** is displayed and then select **Run** or **Generate Report**. Click **OK** when the Criteria box appears and the report will be displayed.

Check that only the account required is shown as opposed to all the nominal accounts. Click on **Print** and choose **OK** from the Print box. Finally select **Close** and **Close** again to return to the main option window.

The examination is now complete.

Chapter 8 | Excersises

Objectives
By the end of the Chapter you wil have practiced

☐

8.1 | Book-keeping and Accounts Level 1

1. M Owens owns a supermarket. The business was started on 1 May. Below is a copy of the Cash Book for the first week.

M Owens
Cash Book

	Cash £	Bank £		Cash £	Bank £
1 May Capital		18500	1 May Equipment		2500
2 May Sales	800		1 May Rent	250	
2 May Cash (contra)		350	1 May Purchases		7300
3 May Sales		600	2 May Bank (contra)	350	
			4 May Delivery Van		6900
			5 May Wages		640
			5 May Drawings		150
			5 May Balances c/d	200	1960
	800	19450		800	19450
6 May Balance b/d	200	1960			

The following invoices were issued and received in respect of a credit sale and a credit purchase.

INVOICE	No: 03
To: P Samuel Date: 4 May	
Business Park	
Southbourne	
From: M Owens	
East Road	
Westbourne	
	£
For: Goods supplied	150

INVOICE	No: 45
To: M Owens Date: 2 May	
East Road	
Westbourne	
From: D Fassam	
Peg Street	
Fishbourne	
	£
For: Goods supplied	75

You are required to:

a) post M Owens Cash Book to the ledger

b) post the invoices to the ledger

c) extract M Owens Trial Balance as at 5 May.

2. D Matthews keeps his Petty Cash Book on the imprest system. The amount of the imprest is £100.

There are four analysis columns.

Stationery
Travel Expenses
Postage
Canteen

PETTY CASH VOUCHER
No 123
Date: 1 November
Required for:
£ p
Postage Stamps 2 00
Signed by: S Emmerson

PETTY CASH VOUCHER
No 124
Date: 4 November
Required for:
£ p
Envelopes 6 60
Signed by: J Kiddle

PETTY CASH VOUCHER
No 125
Date: 6 November
Required for:
£ p
Fruit Juice 8 90
Signed by: P Neve

PETTY CASH VOUCHER
No 126
Date: 9 November
Required for:
£ p
Envelopes 5 20
Signed by: A Haines

PETTY CASH VOUCHER
No 127
Date: 12 November
Required for:
£ p
Pens 1 90
Signed by: P Neve

PETTY CASH VOUCHER
No 128
Date: 14 November
Required for:
£ p
Postage 6 20
Signed by: S Emmerson

```
┌─────────────────────────────────────┐   ┌─────────────────────────────────────┐
│        PETTY CASH VOUCHER           │   │        PETTY CASH VOUCHER           │
│             No 129                  │   │             No 130                  │
│ Date: 19 November                   │   │ Date: 20 November                   │
│                                     │   │                                     │
│ Required for:                       │   │ Required for:                       │
│                    £   p            │   │                    £   p            │
│ Postage            6   20           │   │ Taxi Fare          7   30           │
│                                     │   │                                     │
│ Signed by:  J Kiddle                │   │ Signed by:  S Emmerson              │
└─────────────────────────────────────┘   └─────────────────────────────────────┘

┌─────────────────────────────────────┐   ┌─────────────────────────────────────┐
│        PETTY CASH VOUCHER           │   │        PETTY CASH VOUCHER           │
│             No 131                  │   │             No 132                  │
│ Date: 20 November                   │   │ Date: 24 November                   │
│                                     │   │                                     │
│ Required for:                       │   │ Required for:                       │
│                    £   p            │   │                    £   p            │
│ Taxi Fare          7   30           │   │ Envelopes          8   30           │
│                                     │   │                                     │
│ Signed by:  S Emmerson              │   │ Signed by:  A Haines                │
└─────────────────────────────────────┘   └─────────────────────────────────────┘

┌─────────────────────────────────────┐   ┌─────────────────────────────────────┐
│        PETTY CASH VOUCHER           │   │        PETTY CASH VOUCHER           │
│             No 133                  │   │             No 134                  │
│ Date: 29 November                   │   │ Date: 30 November                   │
│                                     │   │                                     │
│ Required for:                       │   │ Required for:                       │
│                    £   p            │   │                    £   p            │
│ Stationery         7   20           │   │ Milk               2   40           │
│                                     │   │                                     │
│ Signed by:  J Kiddle                │   │ Signed by:  S Emmerson              │
└─────────────────────────────────────┘   └─────────────────────────────────────┘
```

You are required to:

a) enter the opening cash float in the Petty Cash Book at 1 November

b) enter the above vouchers in the Petty Cash Book

c) balance the Petty Cash Book on 30 November. Bring down the balance and restore the imprest.

3. The Cash Book (bank columns only) of R Gold is shown below:

R Gold
Cash Book

		£			£
14 July	Balance b/d	2400	16 July	B Heaton	68
15 July	R Thomas	140	17 July	R Jackson	94
19 July	Sales	630	25 July	W Steele	80
24 July	L Matthews	54	27 July	T Garwood	23

The following statement was issued by the bank:

BANK STATEMENT

NATIONAL BANK
LOCAL BRANCH

In account with: R Gold

All entries to: 31 July are inclusive and complete

Account No 78578924

Date	Detail	Debit £	Credit £	Balance £
14 July	Balance			2400
18 July	R Thomas		140	2540
19 July	B Heaton	68		2472
26 July	Counter credit		630	3102
28 July	W Steele	80		3022
31 July	Bank charges	22		3000
31 July	Tax refund		50	3050

You are required to:

a) Update the Cash Book. Balance the Cash Book on 31 July and bring down the balance.

b) Prepare a Bank Reconciliation Statement as at 31 July.

4. The following Trial Balance was extracted at the end of the financial year 31 January from the books of the business owned by J Elmer.

J Elmer
Trial Balance as at 31 January

	Dr £	Cr £
Cash at bank	4200	
Cash in Hand	530	
Drawings	6900	
Purchases	27860	
Sales		59460
General expenses	1310	
Debtors	1480	
Capital		13280
Electricity	1090	
Creditors		460
Rent	4500	
Fixtures and fittings	8230	
Wages and salaries	10900	
Opening stock	6200	
	73200	73200

Closing stock at 31 January was valued at £3170

You are required to:

a) prepare J Elmer's Trading Account for the year ended 31 January.

b) prepare J Elmer's Profit and Loss Account for the year ended 31 January.

c) prepare J Elmer's Balance Sheet as at 31 January.

1. Adam Lace is a photographer. His Trial Balance at 1 April is as follows:

	Dr £	Cr £
Sales		65810
Purchases	27320	
Stock	3070	
Bank	910	
Cash	300	
Trade Creditors : F Stewart		600
D Abrahams		330
Drawings	1910	
Fixtures and equipment	45000	
Wages	3020	
Advertising	1950	
General expenses	770	
Capital		17510
	84250	84250

Adam Lace received the following invoices in April:

INVOICE	No: 29
To: Adam Lace Ashurst Bridge Waterlooville	Date: 7 Apr
From: F Stewart West Street Havant	£
For: Films	150

INVOICE	No: 67
To: Adam Lace Ashurst Bridge Waterlooville	Date: 15 Apr
From: D Abrahams Chichester Gate Funtington	£
For: Photo Albums	270

INVOICE	No: 45
To: Adam Lace Ashurst Bridge Waterlooville	Date: 20 Apr
From: F Stewart West Street Havant	£
For: Films	730

Adam Lace's bank account for April is as follows:

Bank		£			£
1 Apr	Balance b/d	910	2 Apr	General Expenses	100
6 Apr	Sales	900	3 Apr	F Stewart	600
13 Apr	Sales	300	17 Apr	Cash	450
20 Apr	Sales	1700	23 Apr	F Stewart	700
26 Apr	Capital	1000	25 Apr	Purchases	500

Adam Lace issued the following cash requisitions during April:

Cash Requisition	Cash Requisition
Date: 14 April	**Date**: 30 April
For: General Expenses £30	**For**: Wages £140
Signed: Adam Lace	**Signed:** Adam Lace

You are required to:

a) write up the Purchase Day Book for April

b) write up the following accounts in Adam Lace's ledger for April:

   Cash
   Purchases
   F Stewart

c) prepare Adam Lace's Trial Balance as at 30 April

2. Steve Lavington's Trial Balance shows a difference of £ 90 which has been placed to a Suspense Account. This is due to the following errors:

1) Purchase of goods from Carl Thomas have been correctly entered in the Purchases Account as £230 but have been entered in the personal account as £320.

2) A payment of £80 for electricity has been credited to both the Cash Account and the Electricity Account.

3) The Sales Account has been undercast by £160

In addition the following have still to be recorded:

1) Dave Andrews, a debtor, has gone bankrupt and cannot repay the £410 he owes. This amount is to be written off.

2) A purchase of a delivery van for the business on credit for £500 from Matt Drew had not been entered at all.

You are required to:

a) make the journal entries which would be used to record the matters listed above.

b) write up the Suspense Account, showing how it is cleared by the appropriate entries.

3 The following accounts appear in the Sales Ledger of James Perkins.

Ann Howard

		£			£
1 Mar	Balance b/d	1950	12 Mar	Sales	1000
15 Mar	Sales Returns	420	31 Mar	Balance c/d	2900
22 Mar	Bank	1500			
22 Mar	Discount Allowed	30			
		3900			3900
1 Apr	Balance b/d	2900			

Jane Parr

		£			£
3 Mar	Balance b/d	150	17 Mar	Bank	720
12 Mar	Sales	630	31 Mar	Balance c/d	60
		780			780
1 Apr	Balance b/d	60			

Kevin Barnes

		£			£
3 Mar	Balance b/d	639	17 Mar	Sales	720
12 Mar	Bank	987	22 Mar	Discount Allowed	13
			31 Mar	Balance c/d	893
		1626			1626
1 Apr	Balance b/d	893			

You are required to:

a) redraft any sales ledger account (s) shown above in which errors exist restating the relevant account(s) in full

b) show how the Sales Ledger Control Account would appear for March after correcting the errors. Bring down the balance at 1 April.

c) list the balances on the individual Sales Ledger accounts and agree the total to the balance on the Sales Ledger Control Account.

4 The following balances were extracted from the books of Andrew Blake, a florist at 1 June:

	£
Equipment	4500
Total debtors	5800
Stock	3200
Bank overdraft	1050
Total creditors	5000
Cash in hand	80

As can be seen Andrew Blake had a bank overdraft of £1050 and cash in hand of £80 at 1 June. The bank require him to reduce his overdraft to £500 by the end of the month.

In order to achieve this Andrew Blake carried out the following transactions during the month of June :

June

3   He sold a quarter of his stock at cost for cash

11   He accepts cash for £2500 in full settlement from a debtor who owed £2650. The balance was to be treated as discount.

19   Leigh Ann Smith will lend the business £400 cash, to be repaid in three months time.

21   He paid a creditor by cash £3600 and was allowed a £400 discount.

26   He sold equipment which had cost £800 for £390. A cheque for this amount was received.

30   He transferred sufficient cash into his business bank account to reduce his overdraft to £500.

You are required to:

a) calculate the working capital at 1 June

b) write up the three column Cash Book of Andrew Blake for the month of June

c) calculate the working capital at 30 June

5 Kate Sparrow is a retailer. Her Trial Balance as at 31 October is as follows:

	Dr £	Cr £
Equipment	10000	
Bank		120
Cash	55	
Drawings	1520	
Purchases	12625	
Sales		36320
General expenses	390	
Debtors	800	
Provision for depreciation : Equipment		1000
Capital		6020
Heating & lighting	280	
Creditors		810
Motor Van	15000	
Discount received		300
Wages and salaries	1800	
Opening stock	2100	
	44570	44570

The following additional information is also available at 31 October:

Stock at cost amounted to £1230
Over the year Kate Sparrow took stock for her own use at cost £200
Wages & salaries owing £250
Depreciation is to be provided for as follows:
   Equipment 30% reducing balance method
   Motor van 25 % straight line method
Discount received of £60 has not yet been recorded
A provision for bad debts is to be created at 4% of debtors.

You are required to:

a) prepare Kate Sparrow's Trading, Profit and Loss Account for the year ended 31 October.

b) prepare Kate Sparrow's Balance Sheet as at 31 October.

8.3   Computerised Accounts Level 1

You are employed in the accounts department of SBS Building Supplies Limited, a company which supplies goods to the building trade.

1. Add the following accounts to the Sales Ledger :

   a) Kennedy Builders (Account No KB 3), 21 Hilbury Road, Fareham PO15 4AS
   b) Howard Construction (Account No HC 14) 8 Meliot Rise, Northam SO14 2EF
   c) Blair Services (Account No BS 56) Colden Yard, Chandlers Ford SO53 7JY
   d) Clarke Contractors (Account No CC37) 126 Main Road Eastleigh SO50 5BL
   e) Soames Developments (Account No SD29) Moot Lane Winchester SO21 1TU

2. Add the following accounts to the Purchase Ledger :

   a)   Salisbury Sand (Account No SS48) 20 Rowlings Road, Salisbury SP1 5ZX
   b)   Cowley Cement (Account No CC81) Danes Drive Southampton SO19 3TT
   c)   E Scott Ltd (Account No ES100) Hamble Lane Hamble SO45 6RP
   d)   T Green & Sons (Account No TG39) 235 Kings Way Andover SP10 9AL
   e)   Castleway (Account No CA44) Ashurst Bridge Road Totton SO40 8TU
   f)   Page Traders (Account No PT43) Junction Ind. Est Ower SO51 9HG

3. Create the following accounts in the Nominal Ledger

Name	Nominal Code
Sales –Cement	4000
Sales-Sand	4001
Purchases-Cement	5000
Purchases-Sand	5001
Rent	7100
Electricity	7200
Gas	7201
Telephone	7502

4. Enter the Sales Ledger with the invoices detailed below

SALES BATCH CONTROL

CUSTOMER		INVOICE		NOMINAL	NET	TAX	GROSS
A/C NO	NAME	DATE	NO	CODE	COST £	£	COST £
KB3	Kennedy Builders	8 May	100241	4000	113.31	19.82	133.13
SD29	Soames Developments	13 May	100242	4001	475.25	83.17	558.42
HC14	Howard Construction	15 May	100243	4001	311.00	54.42	365.42
CC37	Clarke Contractors	22 May	100244	4000	218.46	38.23	256.69
BS56	Blair Services	26 May	100245	4000	88.87	15.55	104.42
		CHECK LIST TOTAL					

NB Ensure that you have entered the Check List Totals on the Batch Control above.

5. Howard Construction (Account No HC 14) has returned some damp sand. Access the Sales Ledger and enter the Credit Note as detailed below:

Date	Ref No	Nom Code	Net	Tax	Gross
23 May	1101	4001	102.00	17.85	119.85

6. On 28 May the company receives a cheque (Cheque No 000055) from Kennedy Builders (Account No KB 3)   for the amount of £133.13. Enter this receipt in the Sales Ledger.

7. Enter the Purchase Ledger with the invoices detailed below

SALES BATCH CONTROL

CUSTOMER		INVOICE		NOMINAL	NET	TAX	GROSS
A/C NO	NAME	DATE	NO	CODE	COST £		COST £
CC81	Cowley Cement	2 May	P2071	5000	297.35	52.03	349.38
SS48	Salisbury Sand	3 May	X3678	5001	289.50	50.66	340.16
PT43	Page Traders	6 May	154	7100	250.00	0.00	250.00
TG39	T Green & Sons	17 May	1823	7200	153.29	26.83	180.12
CA44	Castleway	22 May	8080	7201	29.30	5.13	34.43
ES100	E Scott Ltd	24 May	4E345	7502	83.24	14.57	97.81
		CHECK LIST TOTAL					

8. On 29 May the company made a payment by cheque to Salisbury Sand for the amount of £340.16. Enter this payment in the Purchase Ledger.

9. Obtain printout(s) (hard copy) of the Sales Ledger Report(s) to include customer name, address, account reference number, each transaction and the account balance.

10. Obtain printout(s) (hard copy) of the Purchase Ledger Report(s) to include supplier name, address, account reference number, each transaction and the account balance.

11. Print out a Trial Balance.

8.4 | Computerised Accounts Level 2

You are responsible for the computerised accounts of Tool Supplies Ltd.

1) Create Accounts as follows:

CUSTOMER ACCOUNTS (Sales Ledger)

Acc No

			Acc No		
SL201 Name	Hardley Brothers		SL204 Name	Watson Homes	
Address	Chapel Lane		Address	12 Russell Square	
	Fordingbridge			London	
	SP6 2RG			W1D 4HY	

SL202 Name	Tomb Timber		SL205 Name	Solent Housing	
Address	The Bartons		Address	Broyle Road	
	Winchester			Chichester	
	SO23 5BC			PO19 8RW	

SL203 Name	Jarvis Developments		SL206 Name	Wardle Property Co	
Address	Park Way		Address	2 Delucy Avenue	
	Ringwood			Nursling	
	BH24 2SF			SO16 1AZ	

SALES ACCOUNTS

Nominal Account Reference	Item
4000	Sales - Hammers
4001	Sales - Pliers
4002	Sales - Screwdrivers
4003	Sales – Saws
4004	Sales - Chisels
4005	Sales - Spanners
4006	Sales - Trowels

SUPPLIER ACCOUNTS (Purchase Ledger)

Acc No

PL101 Name	Vardy Vision Ltd	
Address	Morrison Way	
	Maindy	
	CF14 6UU	

PL102	Name	Building Bits
	Address	Shire Park
		Welwyn Garden City
		AL7 4AN

PL103	Name	Miles Merchants
	Address	Wallace House
		Yeovil
		BA22 8PT

PL104	Name	Sundfor Services
	Address	Quarry Yard
		Eastleigh
		SO50 3MJ

PURCHASE ACCOUNTS

Nominal Account Reference	Item
5000	Purchases - Hammers
5001	Purchases - Pliers
5002	Purchases - Screwdrivers
5003	Purchases – Saws
5004	Purchases - Chisels
5005	Purchases - Spanners
5006	Purchases - Trowels

NOMINAL ACCOUNTS

5100	Carriage
7200	Electricity
7501	Postage
7502	Telephone
7504	Stationery

2) Michael Thomas, the owner of Tool Supplies Ltd, commenced business on 1 April by introducing capital of £50,000, by depositing £45,000 into the bank and £5,000 into the cash account.

Enter the above transactions into the appropriate accounts.

3) On 2 April Tool Supplies Ltd paid the following expenses by cash:

Postage	£130.00	zero rated for tax
Stationery	£500.00	plus tax of £87.50
Carriage	£603.48	including tax of £89.88

4) A number of Purchase Ledger transactions have occurred.

Use the PURCHASES BATCH CONTROL (at the end) and enter the transactions. Then use the Batch Control to enter them into your computerised accounting system.

INVOICE

Building Bits
Shire Park
Welwyn Garden City
AL7 4AN

Account No: 705
Invoice No: BB786   **Date:** 3 April

Tools Supplies Ltd
Ashurst Road
Totton
SO40 5TE

Order No: 234   **Dated:** 1 April   **TAX REG NO:** 543987

QUANTITY	DESCRIPTION	UNIT PRICE £	NET COST £	TAX £	GROSS £	NOM CODE
1000	Screwdrivers	3.15	3150.00	551.25	3701.25	5002
	Total		3150.00	551.25	3701.25	

INVOICE

Miles Merchants
Wallace House
Yeovil
BA22 8PT

Account No: TS342
Invoice No: INV785   **Date:** 8 April

Tools Supplies Ltd
Ashurst Road
Totton
SO40 5TE

Order No: 104   **Dated:** 3 April   **TAX REG NO:** 093471

QUANTITY	DESCRIPTION	UNIT PRICE £	NET COST £	TAX £	GROSS £	NOM CODE
1000	Hammers	1.75	1750.00	306.25	2056.25	5000
1000	Spanners	2.25	2250.00	393.75	2643.75	5005
	Total		4000.00	700.00	4700.00	

INVOICE

Sundfor Services
Quarry Yard
Eastleigh
SO50 3MJ

Account No: 70
Invoice No: 0910   **Date:** 10 April

Tools Supplies Ltd
Ashurst Road
Totton
SO40 5TE

Order No: 483   **Dated:** 5 April   **TAX REG NO:** 135792

QUANTITY	DESCRIPTION	UNIT PRICE £	NET COST £	TAX £	GROSS £	NOM CODE
300	Chissels	1.25	375.00	65.63	440.63	5004
500	Trowels	1.50	750.00	131.25	881.25	5006
	Total		1125.00	196.88	1321.88	

INVOICE

Sundfor Services
Quarry Yard
Eastleigh
SO50 3MJ

Account No: 70
Invoice No: 0923   **Date:** 12 April

Tools Supplies Ltd
Ashurst Road
Totton
SO40 5TE

Order No: 502   **Dated:** 8 April   **TAX REG NO:** 135792

QUANTITY	DESCRIPTION	UNIT PRICE £	NET COST £	TAX £	GROSS £	NOM CODE
500	Pliers	0.50	250.00	43.75	293.75	5001
	Total		250.00	43.75	293.75	

71

INVOICE

Vardy Vision Ltd
Morrison Way
Maindy
CF14 6UU

Account No: 329T
Invoice No: SO3776   **Date:** 12 April

Tools Supplies Ltd
Ashurst Road
Totton
SO40 5TE

Order No: 39   **Dated:** 9 April   **TAX REG NO:** 975346

QUANTITY	DESCRIPTION	UNIT PRICE £	NET COST £	TAX £	GROSS £	NOM CODE
200	Saws	0.75	150.00	26.25	176.25	5003
	Total		150.00	26.25	176.25	

INVOICE

Building Bits
Shire Park
Welwyn Garden City
AL7 4AN

Account No: 705
Invoice No: BB811   **Date:** 13 April

Tools Supplies Ltd
Ashurst Road
Totton
SO40 5TE

Order No: 256   **Dated:** 11 April   **TAX REG NO:** 543987

QUANTITY	DESCRIPTION	UNIT PRICE £	NET COST £	TAX £	GROSS £	NOM CODE
400	Hammers	1.75	700.00	122.50	822.50	5000
	Total		700.00	122.50	822.50	

INVOICE

Vardy Vision Ltd
Morrison Way
Maindy
CF14 6UU

Account No: 329T
Invoice No: SO3797   **Date:** 24 April

Tools Supplies Ltd
Ashurst Road
Totton
SO40 5TE

Order No: 50   **Dated:** 13 April   **TAX REG NO:** 975346

QUANTITY	DESCRIPTION	UNIT PRICE £	NET COST £	TAX £	GROSS £	NOM CODE
100	Saws	0.75	75.00	13.12	88.12	5003
	Total		75.00	13.12	88.12	

5). A number of Sales Ledger transactions have occurred.

Use the SALES BATCH CONTROL (at the end) and enter the transactions. Then use the Batch Control to enter them into your computerised accounting system.

INVOICE

Tools Supplies Ltd
Ashurst Road
Totton
SO40 5TE

Account No: SL201
Invoice No: 151   **Date:** 18 April

Hardley Brothers
Chapel Lane
Fordingbridge
SP6 2RG

Order No: 39   **Dated:** 9 April   **TAX REG NO:** 975346

QUANTITY	DESCRIPTION	UNIT PRICE £	NET COST £	TAX £	GROSS £	NOM CODE
6	Pliers	5.75	34.50	6.04	40.54	4001
6	Saws	7.00	42.00	7.35	49.35	4003
	Total		76.50	13.39	89.89	

INVOICE

Tools Supplies Ltd
Ashurst Road
Totton
SO40 5TE

Account No: SL204
Invoice No: 152   **Date:** 20 April

Watson Homes
12 Russell Square
London
W1D 4HY

Order No: WH701   **Dated:** 15 April   **TAX REG NO:** 214365

QUANTITY	DESCRIPTION	UNIT PRICE £	NET COST £	TAX £	GROSS £	NOM CODE
24	Hammers	9.99	239.76	41.95	281.71	4000
	Total		239.76	41.95	281.71	

INVOICE

Tools Supplies Ltd
Ashurst Road
Totton
SO40 5TE

Account No: SL202
Invoice No: 153   **Date:** 23 April

Tomb Timber
The Bartons
Winchester
SO23 5BC

Order No: TT578   **Dated:** 17 April   **TAX REG NO:**214365

QUANTITY	DESCRIPTION	UNIT PRICE £	NET COST £	TAX £	GROSS £	NOM CODE
12	Spanners	10.50	126.00	22.05	148.05	4005
	Total		126.00	22.05	148.05	

INVOICE

Tools Supplies Ltd
Ashurst Road
Totton
SO40 5TE

Account No: SL205
Invoice No: 154   **Date:** 23 April

Solent Housing
Broyle Road
Chichester
PO19 8RW

Order No: SH029   **Dated:** 17 April   **TAX REG NO:** 214365

QUANTITY	DESCRIPTION	UNIT PRICE £	NET COST £	TAX £	GROSS £	NOM CODE
20	Screwdrivers	15.75	315.00	55.13	370.13	4002
24	Trowels	7.99	191.76	33.56	225.32	4006
	Total		506.76	88.69	595.45	

INVOICE

Tools Supplies Ltd
Ashurst Road
Totton
SO40 5TE

Account No: SL203
Invoice No: 155   **Date:** 24 April

Jarvis Developments
Park Way
Ringwood
BH24 2SF

Order No: JD21   **Dated:** 18 April   **TAX REG NO:** 214365

QUANTITY	DESCRIPTION	UNIT PRICE £	NET COST £	TAX £	GROSS £	NOM CODE
4	Chisels	7.75	31.00	5.43	36.43	4004
	Total		31.00	5.43	36.43	

INVOICE

Tools Supplies Ltd
Ashurst Road
Totton
SO40 5TE

Account No: SL206
Invoice No: 156   **Date:** 26 April

Wardle Property Co
2 Delucy Avenue
Nursling
SO16 1AZ

Order No: WP455   **Dated:** 20 April   **TAX REG NO:** 214365

QUANTITY	DESCRIPTION	UNIT PRICE £	NET COST £	TAX £	GROSS £	NOM CODE
8	Screwdrivers	15.75	126.00	22.05	148.05	4002
2	Pliers	5.75	11.50	2.01	13.51	4001
	Total		137.50	24.06	161.56	

INVOICE

Tools Supplies Ltd
Ashurst Road
Totton
SO40 5TE

Account No: SL206
Invoice No: 157   **Date:** 27 April

Wardle Property Co
2 Delucy Avenue
Nursling
SO16 1AZ

Order No: WP460   **Dated:** 21 April   **TAX REG NO:**214365

QUANTITY	DESCRIPTION	UNIT PRICE £	NET COST £	TAX £	GROSS £	NOM CODE
5	Chisels	7.75	38.75	6.78	45.53	4004
	Total		38.75	6.78	45.53	

INVOICE

Tools Supplies Ltd
Ashurst Road
Totton
SO40 5TE

Account No: SL205
Invoice No: 158   **Date:** 29 April

Solent Housing
Broyle Road
Chichester
PO19 8RW

Order No: SH045   **Dated:** 23 April   **TAX REG NO:** 214365

QUANTITY	DESCRIPTION	UNIT PRICE £	NET COST £	TAX £	GROSS £	NOM CODE
18	Hammers	9.99	179.82	31.46	211.28	4000
	Total		179.82	31.46	211.28	

6). Tools Supplies Ltd paid the following expenses by cheque on 28 April:

Electricity	Cheque No 100450	£528.75	including tax of 78.75
Telephone	Cheque No 100451	£200.00	plus tax of £35.00

7). Hardley Brothers have returned 2 Saws (invoice number 151) as they were damaged in transit. A credit note ref no 13 has been sent representing a net cost of £14.00 and tax of £2.45.

8). Tools Supplies Ltd paid the following suppliers by cheque on 25 April:

Building Bits	A/c PL102	Cheque No 100452	£4523.75
Miles Merchants	A/c PL103	Cheque No 100453	£4700.00
Sundfor Services	A/c PL104	Cheque No 100454	£1615.63

9). Tools Supplies Ltd received the following cheques from their customers on 30 April:

Tomb Timber	A/c SL202	Cheque No 001110	£148.05
Watson Homes	A/c SL204	Cheque No 222967	£281.71

10). Obtain the following printouts (hard copy) :

a) Sales Ledger Report(s) to include customer name, address, account reference number, each transaction and the account balance.

b) Purchase Ledger Report(s) to include supplier name, address, account reference number, each transaction and the account balance.

c) Bank Account Analysis.

d) A Trial Balance.

PURCHASES BATCH CONTROL

CUSTOMER A/C NO NAME		INVOICE DATE NO	NOMINAL CODE	NET COST	TAX	GROSS COST
				£	£	£
CHECK LIST TOTAL						

SALES BATCH CONTROL

CUSTOMER A/C NO NAME		INVOICE DATE NO	NOMINAL CODE	NET COST	TAX	GROSS COST
				£	£	£
CHECK LIST TOTAL						